Growth and understanding are both led by questions. Yet curious students are often seen as bothersome, naive or even disloyal, as if they exceeded some unspoken quota. Tom Hughes, in his insightful book *Curious*, shatters the false paradigm and invites us to a deeper understanding with questions that shape our faith and future.

> **WAYNE CORDEIRO**
> Author, *Leading on Empty*

Curiosity is a key trait of a person eager to learn, desirous of truth. Tom Hughes has captured the heart of the Kingdom leadership style Jesus modeled that shaped the disciples, confounded the religious, and drew the seekers. In an age inundated with information, may we never lose the wonder that causes us to ask questions about the things that matter most.

> **TAMMY DUNAHOO**
> General supervisor, The Foursquare Church

When I receive a new book, the first question I ask is, "Why should I read this?" Which, according to *Curious*, is the right question to ask. And here is my response: Because Tom Hughes has brilliant insights that will help us more consequentially impact the world. Don't ask, just read.

> **GREG NETTLE**
> President, Stadia Global Church Planting

This book is full of wisdom and freedom! Every leader will walk away with a fresh new perspective that will enable them to not only endure the test of time but do it with lasting joy and purpose.

TOMMY WALKER
Worship leader

Tom has done something a really important with *Curious*. He has lifted the lid on the way Jesus taught. Jesus was a rabbi, and he used a rabbinical "question and answer" model to help people understand the truth. In this marvelous book Tom Hughes has elucidated this method for contemporary Christians. And he's done it in a way that we can all understand! You don't need to be a pastor or theologian to read this book; anyone with a bit of commitment can discover the huge treasury of spiritual truth found within.

MIKE BREEN
Founder and global leader, 3DMovements

This deeply insightful and creative book by Tom Hughes is, I believe, a resource that comes to us directly from the guiding hand of the Holy Spirit! It is not every day that we see such inspired, God-driven works—a tool that echoes and highlights for us the very character traits of Jesus. He who asked the questions that generated life-bearing promise *continues* to do so in our lives. Those who remain sensitive and alert to His penetrating inquiries will reap the rewards of promised fruitfulness. This book helps lead the way!

GLENN C. BURRIS JR.
President, The Foursquare Church

If you want to *really* screw up in leadership, act like you've got it all figured out. If you want to put yourself in the place to lead successfully, read this book!

TIM HARLOW
Pastor, Parkview Church, Chicago

In a world where so many seek to offer neatly wrapped answers, we desperately need to rediscover the simple power of the question. In his brilliant *Curious*, Tom Hughes explores how humble, question-led faith, life, and leadership bring us a depth and integrity that easy platitudes are too insecure to reach.

JO SAXTON
Chair of 3DMovements

CURIOUS

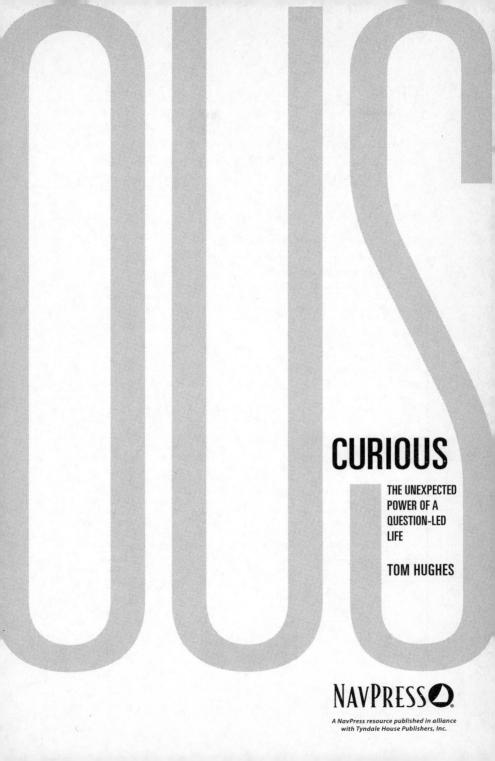

CURIOUS

THE UNEXPECTED POWER OF A QUESTION-LED LIFE

TOM HUGHES

NAVPRESS

A NavPress resource published in alliance
with Tyndale House Publishers, Inc.

NavPress is the publishing ministry of The Navigators, an international Christian organization and leader in personal spiritual development. NavPress is committed to helping people grow spiritually and enjoy lives of meaning and hope through personal and group resources that are biblically rooted, culturally relevant, and highly practical.

For more information, go to www.NavPress.com.

The Team:
Don Pape, Publisher
David Zimmerman, Acquisitions Editor

Cover design by Dean H. Renninger
Interior design by Nicole Grimes

Author photo taken by Bob Palermini, copyright © 2014. All rights reserved.

Published in association with the literary agency of Mark Sweeney & Associates, 28540 Altessa Way, Suite 201, Bonita Springs, FL 34135.

Cataloging-in-Publication Data is available.

ISBN 978-1-63146-343-3

Printed in the United States of America

21	20	19	18	17	16	15
7	6	5	4	3	2	1

To my dad and mom:

Thank you for the foundation you set in me of
knowing I am loved from my earliest years.

To my joyous bride and closest friend, Allison:

Thank you for who you are. You leave everyone you meet
better off than when they first met you. I want to follow
Jesus more wholeheartedly because of you. I love you.

To Mark Pickerill, my Yoda:

Thank you for taking a chance to welcome me into your life.
I am a different man because of your encouragement, prayer,
laughter, and leadership. Everyone should be so fortunate to
have a Mark Pickerill in their lives. I only hope to one day,
in a small way, do for others what you have done for me.

To my Christian Assembly Church family:

Thank you for being a joy to serve. Thank you for being people
who are humble enough to ask prayerful questions and courageous
enough to live into our answers as we follow Jesus together.

To God alone be the glory.

CONTENTS

FOREWORD

As every photographer knows, the lens we choose determines the image we see.

Consider how a wide-angle lens reveals things on the periphery we'd never see otherwise, or how a telephoto lens brings to life details too distant to be seen by the naked eye, or how a well-chosen filter changes our perception and even our feelings about a particular scene or setting.

It's the same with the questions we ask. They reveal things that would otherwise remain unseen and unknown. And that's why good leaders ask lots of questions, even when they think they already know the answers.

Jesus (the ultimate discipler and leader) was asked lots of questions. He obviously knew the answers. But surprisingly, he seldom gave the direct answer his inquirers were hoping for. Most often he responded to their questions with another question, a story, or some other response that forced them to think.

He also initiated lots of conversations with a question. Again, not because he didn't know the answer, but in order to reveal the deepest thoughts, values, and heart intentions of his hearers.

As Tom Hughes so brilliantly points out, Jesus-like questions are in short supply today. We live in a day and age when leaders are expected to provide all the answers—even before anyone asks.

The unfortunate result has been a proliferation of Jesus-followers who hold tightly to all the answers they've been given, but who have never learned to think or follow the leading of Jesus and the Holy Spirit on their own.

They've been taught the "priesthood of the believer." But they've been discouraged from ever practicing it.

That's why I find this book to be so valuable and needed. Tom's insights into question-led discipleship (and his specific questions for self-discovery and for leading others) are incredibly helpful.

Even if you understand the value of questions, his perspective and unique filter will help you see things you've not seen before. It did for me, and I'm confident it will do the same for you.

If you lead anything (a family, a small group, a ministry, or perhaps a group of employees, a department, or even an entire company), this book will help you lead better because it will help you ask better questions of both yourself and others. Questions that will reveal things you've probably not seen before.

Larry Osborne
Author and Pastor, North Coast Church

INTRODUCTION

"Stop asking so many questions. Your problem is that you are too curious."

I remember the moment clearly.

I was a student in high school and had signed up to go on a ski trip that was the collaboration of several different churches' student ministries. The hour-long drive to the ski resort allowed for some time to talk, and a small handful of us students got into a conversation with the two youth pastors on our bus. Normal chatter turned to questions of the meaning of life, God, Jesus, how prayer worked, why there was suffering in the world, if the Bible could be trusted, and more.

At that time in my life, I was not certain what I believed, or if I believed, in any god, let alone the God of the Bible. I had a lot of questions, and we had an hour to kill.

I was not alone in my questions. Some of the other students also chimed in with their own questions; others weighed in with their thoughts on the questions that were raised. But the responses of the two leaders could not have been more different.

One youth pastor was from a different church than the one I attended. He rebuked me for my questions. For him, it may have only been a passing comment; for me it was a flashbulb memory—the kind of memory that sticks with you in vivid detail.

Unable, unwilling, or uninterested in wrestling with the questions being bantered about, he gave up on the conversation and moved to another part of the bus. I moved on from the rebuke to enjoy the rest of the trip, largely because of the response of the other youth pastor who was present.

Jerry was the youth pastor of the church I attended. He stayed with us, sitting and listening as the questions kept coming. Sometimes he replied to a question with a probing question of his own, wanting to know why the question was so important to us. Other times, he answered what he could, shared from his own experiences, and sometimes simply said, "I don't know. I've wondered that same thing at times." Simply staying with us in our questions was a powerful symbolic act.

For that first youth pastor, a life of faith in God and a steady stream of questions are like putting ketchup on a bowl of cereal. They just aren't meant to go together. In his view, it's best to keep them apart. In his world, curiosity not only killed the cat, it can kill faith in Jesus. I have found that nothing could be further from reality. Jerry showed me that not every question needs to be answered in perfect detail in order to trust that God is real and will help us lead the lives he created us to live. Jerry is one of the people who showed me that faith isn't always about having airtight arguments and answers; more often faith is about living your way into questions as they come up, trusting God to guide you along the way.

How our theology shapes our biography, and how our biography shapes our theology, is mysterious at times. The importance of asking questions to discover what is true or real has a long history. Socrates was so famous for his use of questions to illuminate ideas that his style of curiosity became known as the Socratic method. However, even Socrates noted his limitations. Socrates' foundation was that as a teacher, "I know that I know nothing."[1] Any wisdom that he had was gained through the communal questioning of his disciples. Socrates was searching for what has been called the logic of reality—that is, the logic that undergirds the truest reality.

Four hundred years after Socrates died, the logic that Socrates was searching for was discovered, but not as a proposition; it was born as a baby. The language that the Gospel writers use to capture the incarnation of Jesus is stunning. Luke's Gospel captures Zechariah's prophecy from the Holy Spirit: "Praise the Lord, the God of Israel, because he has visited and redeemed his people" (Luke 1:68). The word translated "visited" in Greek is *epeskepato*—a combination of *skepato*, from which we get the English word "skeptic," and *epe*, a prefix that means to move toward something or someone with helpful intent. In other words, Jesus' incarnation shows us that God moves toward skeptics with the intent to help.

The logic of all life was born in Bethlehem. The Gospel of John seeks to capture the meaning of the incarnation by telling us that in the beginning was the *logos*, translated "Word" (John 1:1) and from which we get the English word "logic." What does it mean for us to hear that the Incarnation is, in essence, the logic of all life coming toward skeptics with helpful intent?

As Jesus grew up, it became clear that he was greater than Socrates. Jesus never said, "I know that I know nothing," but rather, "I am the way, the truth, and the life" (John 14:6). Jesus was not limited to whatever wisdom and insight he could gain through questioning those around him. Instead, Jesus is himself the wisdom and insight that we are looking for in our questions. If there was ever someone who had the right to rebuke us for our questions, it is Jesus. And yet, as we will see, Jesus was the master of asking questions—yet not because he did not know the answer. Something else is going on here. There's something about what he wants to shape in us that is not simply about getting the right answers in our heads, but living the right answers with our lives.

Curious is penned with two sets of people in mind. The first group is those who simply want to discover what it looks like to follow Jesus in everyday life. The launching point for each chapter is a question worth asking. Each of us has strengths and limitations that God has given to us; they help us discover the story he has in mind to write through our questions and the answers that flow from his bigger story of redemption. When we humbly ask God our questions, we unleash his power to help us live into the life he created us to live.

The second group I have in mind with this book is those who not only want to grow in their own followership of Jesus, but who want to help others within their realm of influence do the same. These people may or may not have titles; they may be pastors, small group leaders, dads or moms. I call these people leaders, and I am convinced that most people are leaders in the lives of at least a handful of other people. The moment you desire to use your influence to move someone with you toward Christ is the moment that you become a leader.

Almost all the people I know in leadership got their start by watching someone else. Those are usually the good stories. However, I also know a much greater number of people who never stepped into formal leadership of any sort. Usually, when I talk with these people, they tell me stories of coming to the conclusion that they could not possibly ever lead others. When you ask them why they have come to that decision, their answers are revealing. Many saw someone leading and thought, *I will never have the confidence they have. I will never know enough to lead like they do. I will never be able "get a vision" like they do.* Do not sideline the influence God has given you simply because you fear that you do not know all the answers. Maybe you need to instead be willing to ask the right questions.

The lines between these two audiences blur, so at times the chapters of *Curious* do the same. You will also notice that I do not address many of the classic questions that come up on the way to initial faith in Christ. There are many great books that address those questions.[2] But this book is about asking questions that result in answers that are not so much written down as they are lived out. They are generative questions designed to help us ask our way to the world God wants. In other words, how does trusting the logic of all life lead me to incarnate my trust in him?

The book is organized in two sections. The first section helps us see just how often Jesus used questions to provoke and stir faith in people's lives. Questions are not the antagonist to faith, but actually the way to a more integrated everyday faith in Christ. This section also explores the power of the right questions in the life of those who seek to influence others toward life in Christ. A final chapter in this section considers how the right questions unleash creative momentum among groups of people toward living into the world God wants.

The second section of *Curious* is a set of questions that I have found to be worth asking in my own everyday follower-ship of Jesus. They are questions that we ask God in prayer. For those of you who desire to influence others toward Christ, I encourage you to ask these questions first for your-self. From there, we are better equipped to help others ask them and live into the answers God has designed for each one of us uniquely. At the end of each chapter are some questions worth being curious about to help you reflect on your own or discuss with a small group.

The logic of all life became flesh and dwelt among us with helpful intent. He often taught, led, and helped people live into the lives we were created for through the power of the right questions. A curious faith helps us discover and live into God's desire for us and our world. Curiosity may have killed the cat, but it does wonders for living into the world God wants with us.

WHY QUESTIONS MATTER FOR THE LIFE OF FAITH

PART 1

1

THE UNEXPECTED POWER OF THE RIGHT QUESTION: JESUS' MOST COMMON LEADERSHIP METHOD

A sudden bold and unexpected question does many times surprise a man and lay him open.

FRANCIS BACON

What are you looking for?

JESUS, IN JOHN 1:38 (HCSB)

I WISH YOU COULD EACH spend a week with Dr. Gregg.

Dr. Gregg was my high school physics teacher, an extremely nice man with one frustrating habit: He would *always* answer a question with a question. On lab days the room would be filled with high-school students running physics experiments, using items such as a marble and a ramp to make discoveries about mass, momentum, velocity, and acceleration. Sometimes we would send the same marble down the same ramp with the same height, and we would get a different result. We were in high school; none of us knew how it all worked.

A constant line of students would approach Dr. Gregg's desk with frustrated questions.

"I did the exact same thing twice. Why did I get a different result?"

"I don't understand why this is happening."

"The formula that we learned doesn't seem to be applying in this case. Why not?"

We hoped for answers, but Dr. Gregg just offered us questions.

"Why do *you* think you got a different result?"

"What do you think may be a different way to approach the experiment?"

"Why do *you* think the formula you learned is not applying in this instance?"

Dr. Gregg was frustrating, irritating, and even enraging at times, but he was also memorable, because he would not play our game. "Look, just tell us the answers so we can know what to put on the test when it comes." He provoked us not just to learn, but also to learn how to learn. He did not simply want us to regurgitate answers; he wanted us to ask the right kinds of questions.

I think Dr. Gregg was a bit like Jesus.

The Master of Question-Led Leadership

Jesus did not hold many question-and-answer sessions. More often he held question-and-question sessions. His response to a question was often simply another question. Throughout the four Gospels of Jesus, he is asked 183 questions. Of those 183 questions, how many do you think he answered directly? Four. He responds to the other 179 questions with a question, a parable, or a cryptic remark that leaves those gathered with even more questions.

I'd imagine that right now some of you are thinking, *Well, what are the four questions that Jesus answers directly?* But I can hear the voice of Dr. Gregg: "Don't tell them! They will learn more if you ask them a question." So, what four questions do *you* think Jesus answered directly?[1]

Clearly, questions were not the *only* way that Jesus taught or led people. He used many different ways to do that. He confronted some people with very direct words. Other times he launched into decisive action. Other times he did various miracles that testified to his words. Still other times he gave long sermons that were designed to help instruct large crowds of people. And yet, woven through Jesus' story is the recurring theme of asking questions to those he encountered.

Judging by the way he interacted with people, Jesus was not as committed to up-front clarity as we are. We can slide into thinking that Jesus is interested in always and only ensuring that we have the right answers. The reality turns out to be somewhat different. He seems more interested in ensuring that we are considering the right questions. In fact, if we include the questions that Jesus puts in the mouths of characters in his parables, Jesus himself asks an astounding 307 questions in the Gospels.[2] This can be an eye-opening bit of information if you have thought that Jesus was interested in only giving clear answers or resolving people's dilemmas in life. Jesus created as many dilemmas as he solved for people.

Jesus upends our modern infatuation with clarity. The modern school of thought is that the clearest person in the room, the one who defines reality in the most compelling way, is the one we should listen to and follow. We organize ourselves around clear vision statements, clear mission statements, and clear core values. Certainly, there is some value to clarity. However, the shadow side of clarity is that it creates consumers, not disciples. And a consumer mind-set ends the generative, creative process of the spreading of Kingdom of God.

Jesus wants us to be his disciples, but that is the not the end of it. He then invites us to *make* disciples too (Matthew 28:18-20). Discipleship is to see and hear who God is and what genuine reality is as God reveals it, and then to live our lives according to that reality. Maybe that's why Jesus so often declares, "Whoever has ears, let them hear" (Matthew 13:9, NIV; see also Mark 4:23; Luke 14:35; and elsewhere). To his disciples he says, "Blessed are your eyes because they see, and your ears because they hear" (Matthew 13:16, NIV).

I'm reminded of my days in my high school mathematics class when it was not enough to simply provide the correct answer to a question. In the words of my math teacher, we had to "show our work." That phrase meant we had to be able to explain *how* we arrived at our conclusion. The process mattered because how we found an answer applied to questions we would encounter later on. Discipleship is the act of "showing our process," not just having the right answers. I might know the "right" answer because I heard it somewhere, but I will not actually live from that answer until I ask the soul questions that help that answer become *my* answer.

Our modern model of learning seems set on getting ready for a test. Jesus was not interested in getting the right answer *out* of people as much as he was interested in getting the right answer *into* people. The best way to do that is by asking a focused question at the right time. As John Claypool once observed:

> Jesus realized that most people are not just empty vessels into which one pours answers directly. If a truth is going to make any difference in a person's life, it is going to have to connect with where that person is already. Therefore, answering an inquiry by a further question is a way of probing the questioner more deeply, finding out exactly what is on their minds, and getting them involved in finding the answer they are seeking.[3]

Jesus' questions are often unsettling. His questions are not idle. They lead us. They provoke us. When we offer only answers to those who don't know Jesus, there is no space for them to deeply integrate the *implications* of who Jesus is and what he has done. They are not forced to wrestle with it, to digest it.

A Simple Question That Is Hard to Answer

Even with his very first followers, Jesus led by questions. He asked them something so simple that it is hard to comprehend, let alone attempt to answer.

The scene opens with John the Baptist and two (at first unnamed) followers (John 1:35-37). Up to this point, John was the man on the scene. He was the media sensation of the day. People looked to John for spiritual guidance and would come out from the towns and cities in droves to see him, hear him teach, and be baptized in the Jordan River.

It would have been easy for John to cling to center stage a bit longer. But he doesn't. John does two remarkable things.

First, he recognizes what God is doing around him—namely, that his half-cousin, Jesus, is the Lamb of God that takes away the sin of the world.

Second, he chooses to get on board with God's agenda.

Great leadership not only knows when the time is right to take the reins; it also knows when the time is right to let them go. John knows his time is coming to a close, and he refuses to let his ego keep the spotlight on himself. John points people to Jesus at the expense of his crowd shrinking. The time has come for him to decrease so that Jesus might increase in the eyes of the people (John 3:30).

John tells his two followers, essentially, "Stop following me. Go and follow Jesus. Jesus is the Lamb of God." This is a decree—not very question-led. Declarations have their purpose; they can be incredibly valuable. But often their purpose is to get the process of investigation and questioning moving forward. What follows after John's decree, for both him and his followers, is interesting. John eventually is imprisoned and moves from clarity to curiosity, as he asks Jesus, "Are You the One who is to come, or should we expect someone else?" (Matthew 11:2-3, HCSB). In other words, "Was I right or was I wrong when I earlier said you were the Lamb of God?" Jesus doesn't respond with a question, but neither does he respond with a decree. Instead, he gives John more to think about: "The blind see, the lame walk, . . . the dead are raised, and the poor are told the good news. And if anyone is not offended because of Me, he is blessed" (Matthew 11:5-6, HCSB).

In the case of John's two disciples, hearing that Jesus is the Lamb of God does not give them an immediate life-changing faith. Instead, it mainly sets the stage for a three-year investigation of John's claim and its implications for their lives. John's faith is enough to get them going, but it's not enough to keep them going. Along the way they will need to ask their questions and wrestle with John's conclusion to see if they too can come to that same trust. That investigation begins with their first direct encounter with Jesus.

When Jesus turned and noticed them following
Him, He asked them, "What are you looking for?"
JOHN 1:38, HCSB

"What are you looking for?" is really a simple question, isn't it? What astounds me is that the first question Jesus asks those who would follow him is not about sin, brokenness, politics, or family history. It is not even a question about God or what we believe God is like. It is a question that gives us a glimpse of the heart of God. It's a question that also stops us to give us a glimpse into ourselves.

"What are you looking for?" is a stunning question—brilliant in its simplicity, vexing in its answer. Jesus does not tell them what they are looking for, or even direct them toward what they *should* be looking for; he asks them, and by asking them, he leads them (and us). We are all in search of something. We are all on a quest. Jesus invites their internal, unspoken reality to the surface with a single question. At the very core, it is the foundational question of discipleship, of leadership, of life. What are you looking for?

By asking his first disciples that simple question, Jesus alerts us that he is not some systematic theologian walking around teaching dogmas so that we can pass some heavenly multiple-choice exam at the pearly gates. By asking that simple question, Jesus is offering these two men conversation, engagement, relationship, thinking, wrestling, and soul awareness. By asking that simple question, Jesus wants to unearth something in us. We cannot answer that question without exploring our heart and soul a bit. The moment that particular question takes root in us we become students of what matters most to us in life. Only once we have wrestled with that question can we even compare it to what Jesus might suggest we begin to look for with our lives.

The right question can do that. The Trappist monk Thomas Merton once reflected:

> God, my God, . . . with You it is always the same thing! Always the same question that nobody knows how to answer! . . . While I am asking questions which You do not answer, You ask me a question which is so simple that I cannot answer. I do not even understand the question.[4]

The opening question to these first disciples of Jesus is an invitation to take stock of their lives. It's an invitation to a holy pause. The question stops us long enough to take measure of whether the activity of our lives matches the deepest desires of our heart. Each of us must answer that question, and the earlier in life the better. There may be no greater tragedy than a life spent looking for the wrong thing. We all know people who have spent much of their life believing they were looking for something, only to find it, achieve it, buy it, or gain it and then realize it was not what they were actually looking for. It did not fill the void or end the quest. As the great theologian Bono once sang, "I still haven't found what I'm looking for."

Discovering What We Are Truly Looking For

Chris Brady and Orrin Woodward share a story in their book *Launching a Leadership Revolution* that is so helpful that it's worth repeating.

> The legend is told of a young squire in the service of a great knight. The squire's lifelong ambition is someday to become a knight himself. Through the years, the knight trains the squire in techniques of battle and weaponry. Being young, the squire is impatient and is prone to ask the knight if he, the squire, is ready to officially become a knight yet. Tiring of these repeated questions, the great knight sends his squire high into the hills to seek out an old sage who had once been the greatest knight of all.

The squire finds the sage and announces what he wants: to become a knight. The sage silently leads the squire to a lake, where they board a boat and set out. When they reach the lake's center, the sage instructs the squire to get into the water. A little dubiously, the squire jumps into the frigid water.

> Before the boy can reemerge, the sage reaches in the water and grabs the squire's head, holding him under. The squire kicks furiously and grabs at the still strong arm of the sage, but to no avail. The seconds drag into minutes, and finally the fight

is all but gone out of the squire. At that instant,
the sage lifts the boy back into the boat.

The squire is furious and demands an explanation, which the
sage calmly provides.

"When I had you submerged, what was going
through your mind?"
    The squire thought for a moment, his anger
subsiding a bit.
    "Air, I thought. Air. I've got to get air or I'll die.
That's all I was thinking."
    The sage replied, "There you have it, then, young
squire. When you want to be a knight as badly as
you wanted that air, you'll become one."[5]

Sometimes desperation is the key to understanding what really
matters to you. Discovering what we are each truly looking for
is no small task, but it is possible. It often includes many false
starts and restarts. However, if we stick with it, with God's help
we can genuinely discover what we are looking for.

What Is Your Air?

Jesus' opening question to the first two disciples is like the
sage and the squire. He is asking what they are looking for—
what is their air? In time he will ask how desperately they
want what they are looking for.[6]

One of these two men is named Andrew (some believe the other is the disciple named John, though we are never told specifically). In response to Jesus' question, they address him as "Rabbi," which means "Teacher." Though they have been John the Baptist's disciples, they are now in effect positioning themselves as Jesus' students, his disciples.

The word *disciple* means student, learner, or apprentice. God created us to be learners, and we are all learning from someone. Someone's thoughts, someone's teaching, someone's view of the way things "really are" in the "real world" is shaping how we do life, shaping our view of what matters in life, what is real in life. Someone is filling in the answer of what we are looking for and how to find it.

Oftentimes, the teachings we are conditioned by are filtered and spread through culture. In effect, our discipleship is usually not through a direct one-on-one relationship with a personal mentor as much as being bathed in the constant culture of thoughts that we are inundated with each day. Some of these might actually reinforce the teachings of Jesus, but of course, not all of them do. Some are in direct opposition to what the logic of all life taught and how he lived. It's not a matter of whether or not we will become a disciple. We already are. The only question is whose disciple we will be.

We expect students to ask the questions, but here the rabbi asks questions as well. Jesus' call to be his disciples is not a call from non-discipleship to discipleship. It's a call to switch rabbis. You are free to learn from anyone, but you are not free to learn from no one. We were created for discipleship.

Of course, we can learn from more than one person. When those people or ideas part ways, the story of our lives will tell whose disciples we are, whether we ever articulated that choice or not. As Jesus once revealed, "No one can serve two masters. For you will hate one and love the other; you will be devoted to one and despise the other" (Luke 16:13). If we are not a disciple of Jesus, then we are learning and accepting someone's answer to the question "What are you looking for?" and making it our own.

The two men do not immediately have an articulated answer to the question; however, they start to live into the question the moment it is asked.

A Question with an Invitation

I live in the city of Los Angeles, a city filled with people from seemingly every nation and every part of the United States. We are all looking for something. "What are you looking for?" is a foundational question of life because we will wrap the days, priorities, and agendas of our lives around its answer. It's safe to say that most of us are looking for things like security, significance, belonging, and love. Depending on whom we listen to, we will try to find those things in any manner of ways. If we trust that money is our security, then we will try to save our way to salvation. In looking for love, we will try to become what another person finds lovable. We all are looking for something—often a cluster of things. The question becomes how do we actually find it.

Jesus does not tell his first two disciples what they are looking for or even how to get it. The logic of all life asks a question that begins to open their eyes and put flesh on their hope. He comes close to them to help them in their search. That same question today leads us to consider if we even know what we are looking for, and whether our lives match up to our quest. What we are looking for can be a moving target in our hearts.

In response to Jesus' question, Andrew and the other disciple ask, "Where are you staying?" (John 1:38). Seems like they fumbled that opportunity if you ask me. How about "John the Baptist said you were the Lamb of God. We are searching for the Lamb of God. Are you the Lamb of God or not?" Maybe they were being polite, were caught off guard, or were even a bit afraid. Maybe they were thinking, *Now that you ask that question, I realize I have no idea what I am looking for.* Instead they ask Jesus where he is staying.

For his part, Jesus follows his original question with an invitation: "Come and see." The Oxford don C. S. Lewis once remarked:

We can make people (often) attend to the Christian point of view for half an hour or so; but the moment they have gone away from our lecture or laid down our article, they are plunged back into a world where the opposite position is taken for granted. As long as that situation exists, widespread success is simply impossible.[7]

This is a challenge for any teaching that is primarily based on information rather than relationships or lifestyle. I can know that it might be a good idea for me to lose some weight, I can know that this happens when I consume fewer calories than I expend, but the best guarantee of weight loss seems to be relationships with others who live in such ways to maintain a healthy weight. Information alone is not enough. It requires relationship.

"Come and see." Those three words are pregnant with meaning, possibility, an opportunity for something more than just an answer. He could have given them the address where he was staying. But Jesus' invitation shows them that he actually wants to *be* with them. In one short interaction, Jesus moves from a question that invites us to explore our lives and hearts, to an invitation to explore *his* life and heart.

Jesus is the master at leading us with questions. We are obsessed with clarity and answers. He often answers our questions by being intentionally vague. Maybe because he was interested in something more than people who could regurgitate the right answers but live the wrong lives. Maybe he knew that many of us don't even know what we are looking for. He seems to be aware that we often tend to look for the right things in the wrong places and in the wrong ways. Maybe he knows what we are looking for even if we do not. Maybe that's why he welcomes us: "Come and see."

The Power of Questions

Jesus was the greatest leader to ever enter history. He could have led in any manner he chose. Certainly, he led in different ways in different situations, but he most often chose to lead people with questions. Whether he was dealing with his closest friends or large crowds, whether dealing with men or women, young or old, rich or poor, sick or healthy, Jews or Gentiles, he asked questions. Even in his first interactions with his rising leaders-in-the-making, he asked a question. Cultivating curiosity might not be a new way to live and lead, but considering how often Jesus did it, it may be the best way.

One of the greatest gifts of humbly asking questions is the freedom to stop pretending that you know it all. We'll take a look at that next.

Questions Worth Being Curious About

1. How would you respond to Jesus' question: What are you looking for?

2. As you think about your life right now, what is your air? Do you want that to be your air or do you wish you were desperate for something different?

3. Is there anywhere in your life that Jesus is responding to the questions you are asking in your heart with an invitation to "come and see"? If so, what first step can you take to respond to his invitation?

2

UNINTENDED PRETENDERS: HOW GOD RESCUES US WITH THE RIGHT QUESTIONS

The important thing is to not stop questioning.

ALBERT EINSTEIN

Do you love me more than these?

JESUS, IN JOHN 21:15

SOMETIMES THE BEST OF THINGS start from the worst of moments.

Like most people, when I entered ninth grade, I wanted to fit in and have friends. One day early in the school year, I was sitting at a lunch table with some of the guys I knew from past years, a few guys who were new to me, and some girls that we each knew as well. There are few social settings as fraught with insecurities (shown as bravado) as coed ninth graders eating lunch at one table.

One guy, whom I had only met in passing, was talking about some of his favorite bands. The first several bands were fairly popular; we all knew their songs. Then he began to talk about his favorite band: Shiloh Blue. He talked about their lyrics and named about three different song titles as his favorite. I was sitting with the group, listening and nodding my head in agreement.

Casually, the guy turned to me and asked, "So Tom, have you ever heard of Shiloh Blue?"

"Yep," I replied.

He named off three of their most popular songs. "Have you heard those?"

I tried to play it cool. "I'm not really *that* into Shiloh Blue, but sure, I've heard those songs."

That's when he dropped a bomb on me. "No, you haven't heard of Shiloh Blue! That's a name for a band that I just made up on the spot. They are a fake band. All the songs I just named are also fakes that I just made up, too.

"But most of all, *you* are a fake. You said you had heard of Shiloh Blue when you never have. You said you heard of their songs when you never had. Ha!"

He called my bluff. He was right. I had gotten caught in a lie. He had set me up and exposed me as a fake.

I never intended to lie. But when the moment came, with the pressure to simply want to fit in, I did. With each question I could feel the hole I was digging get deeper and deeper, but it felt like there was no way out. I had gotten caught up, and he caught me.

I was hoping to be saved by the closing lunch bell, but it never rang. I guess I needed something greater than a bell to save me.

The Honest, More Honest, and Most Honest Versions of Our Story

Over the past couple of decades, I've had the privilege to work with and listen to people from a wide range of life. I've sat with men, women, and students from inside the United States and from other countries. Some of them have been incredibly wealthy or extremely well-educated, while others have been incredibly poor or with limited formal education. One thing I have observed is that within all this diversity, it seems that all people have three versions to our story: *the honest version, the more honest version, and the most honest version.*

Years ago, I sat in a circle with a group of men. It was one of our first times together, although we had committed to be together for a year to grow in our relationships with Christ. On this first week, the main goal was simply to tell a bit about our stories to one another, an icebreaker of sorts.

I set the stage by mentioning the three versions of our story, and the first several men went one by one telling a bit of either their honest or more honest story. Then came a man I will call Sean. Sean took the leap and told the most honest version.

Sean started out by saying that he had a great job and a wonderful family and wife, and he was generally content in life. Then he peeled back another layer. "The more honest version of my story is that though I am generally content, I sometimes wonder if there is more to life and if I am missing something." Then he took it a step further. "The most honest version is that I feel attracted to one of my coworkers. In fact, the most honest version is that I crossed a line and kissed her after work today before coming here to this group." At that, Sean broke down in tears.

That circle felt like holy ground. We were able to speak with Sean, pray with him, and thankfully he chose to break off any contact with the coworker.

The effect on the other men who had already told their stories was palpable. In fact, unable to handle the solemnity of the moment, several of them joked that they wanted a "do over." As the facilitator, I offered them the chance to do just that: to tell the most honest version of their story rather than simply the honest or more honest version. Each of them took advantage of the offer.

The honest version of our story is usually the first version we tell. Since we are not certain how well we can trust those who are listening, this version of our story is highly edited to make us look good, fit in, or avoid the pain of those aspects of our story we wish weren't true. Sometimes there are good reasons to leave out details of our story at the beginning of a relationship, but once trust grows and we are willing to take a risk, then we move to the more honest version of the story, filling in some of the parts we omitted at first. The most humbly courageous people I know move from telling the more honest version to telling the most honest version. We all have an in-built fear of telling this version of our story. And this fear is only compounded when we are invited into greater authority and responsibility. With leadership comes pressure. The stakes are raised. There is a constant pressure to be and do bigger, better, faster, and higher, to be something we are not. It comes from pressures we place on ourselves and from pressures that others place on us. Over a long period of time, the pressure can contort and conform even the most well-intentioned men and women. The pressure comes from always telling the edited versions of our story, and never taking the risk of letting anyone know the most honest version of us in our current state.

It's dangerous ground for our souls; we can slide into becoming unintended pretenders.

Unintended pretending is what happens when you act in small or large ways as though you know more than you know, can do more than you can do, or can deliver more than you actually can deliver. Unintended pretenders project more confidence and security than they actually have. There is something about stepping into moments of pressure, whether the pressure to fit in or the pressure of leadership, that can set the stage for becoming an unintended pretender. Clearly, we are responsible for our ethical choices such as lying, but most people never set out to end up as an unintended pretender. We don't premeditate every lie; sometimes we simply crack under the pressure.

I never started out that fateful ninth-grade day with the goal of deceiving people; but the pressure to fit in was greater than my courage to be honest. Becoming an unintended pretender just kind of happens when we are not paying attention. As the muse Dave Matthews once wrote, "We are making plans to change the world, while the world is changing us."

Even the most ardent followers of Jesus can become unintended pretenders. It's not something new. In fact, it happened two thousand years ago to one of Jesus' closest apprentices.

A Follower Who Became a Leader Who Became an Unintended Pretender

Peter was a regular, everyday fisherman. One day, Peter heard and responded to Jesus' call, "Come, follow me, and I will show you how to fish for people!" (Matthew 4:18-20). Jesus' initial invitation was noticeably lacking in the clarity we often think marks a visionary leader. He did not explain where they would be going. He did not explain what it meant to follow him. He did not even explain what it meant to fish for people or how to do it. Still, Peter took the bait.

For some time after that, Peter was one of many followers of Jesus. A little later, Jesus appointed Peter to be one of his twelve core leaders (Matthew 10:2), and still later, Jesus took this leadership group on a trip to a town named Caesarea Philippi. There Peter received a remarkable affirmation by Jesus. Here is how Matthew recounts the story.

> When Jesus came to the region of Caesarea Philippi,
> he asked his disciples, "Who do people say that the
> Son of Man is?"
>
> "Well," they replied, "some say John the Baptist,

some say Elijah, and others say Jeremiah or one of the other prophets."

Then he asked them, "But who do you say I am?"

Simon Peter answered, "You are the Messiah, the Son of the living God."

Jesus replied, "You are blessed, Simon son of John, because my Father in heaven has revealed this to you. You did not learn this from any human being. Now I say to you that you are Peter (which means 'rock'), and upon this rock I will build my church, and all the powers of hell will not conquer it. And I will give you the keys of the Kingdom of Heaven. Whatever you forbid on earth will be forbidden in heaven, and whatever you permit on earth will be permitted in heaven."

MATTHEW 16:13-19[1]

Once again we see Jesus using his most-repeated way of leading people: by asking questions. Jesus knew the answers to his questions, and yet he chose to use questions to lead Peter to the answer. In that way, this is not a story of Jesus' dictation, but Peter's profession.

With Peter's profession of faith, he was becoming a leader of leaders within the group of twelve. So far, so good. Let's fast-forward to near the end of the Gospel accounts. On their way to the Mount of Olives, Jesus told his twelve disciples, "Tonight all of you will desert me. For the Scriptures say,

'God will strike the Shepherd, and the sheep of the flock will be scattered.'" In that moment, Peter declared his intentions: "Even if everyone else deserts you, I will never desert you" (see Matthew 26:31-35).

Peter was certain he could live by his self-manufactured answers. He believed he could handle the pressure. Maybe he felt like he needed to be strong for Jesus. Maybe he felt like he needed to project confidence for the others in the community of Jesus. Whatever the reason, Peter projected confidence that he would follow through with his good intentions, even if everyone else failed.

Jesus knew better. Peter was about to be revealed as an unintended pretender.

After Jesus was arrested, Peter followed at a distance, arriving at the courtyard of the high priest's home, where Jesus was being beaten and spat upon (Matthew 26:67-75). The pressure had been ratcheted up, and when the moment came to either stand out or fit in, Peter chose to fit in. Three times, each time with increasing intensity, he lied, denying his association with Jesus. When his declaration of faithfulness was sifted, he was found to be a pretender.

Peter learned something about himself. When he left his nets to follow Jesus, he never envisioned this being part of his story. When Jesus chose him as one of the core twelve follower-leaders in this new movement, Peter never imagined this being part of the future. When he made his famous declaration of faith—that Jesus is the Messiah, with Jesus' affirmation of Peter and his profession—he was riding high. But the pressure won. It revealed what was inside of him. He could not live up to his own billing.

Peter learned something about himself. The bad news is that what he learned was not so pretty. The good news, however, is that he would soon learn something about Jesus, too. We will come back to that later.

The Cost of Being an Unintended Pretender

I never planned to serve as a leader of a local church. To me, being a pastor meant working nights, weekends, and holidays—you know, the shifts that everyone wants to avoid at all costs. As I neared the completion of my undergraduate training, I had set my sights on law school and had been accepted. However, during my senior year of college, God redirected my life in ways only God is able to do. I decided that it was worthwhile to spend a year to explore what I felt and others affirmed might be God's call on my life, and I ended up receiving an invitation to move to Charleston, South Carolina, to start a ministry to middle-school and high-school students in a local church of a couple hundred adults on a Sunday morning.

The honest version of the story was that I felt and others affirmed my call to start that ministry. The more honest version of the story is that I really had no idea what I was doing. I had graduated from a secular university, with no training for ministry leadership. The *most* honest version of my story is that I vacillated between sheer terror and the mantra "Fake it till you make it." I thought it would be hard to start a ministry from scratch, but I was wrong. It was brutally hard. The elders and senior leaders were very supportive, but leading anything is hard, and leading something you are starting from scratch is harder.

I led the student ministries of that church for a number of years. There were many times I projected a much greater sense of confidence than I actually felt or had. I did it with volunteers, with students, with parents, and with members of the church. For some reason, I thought that was what leaders do, at least successful leaders. I thought that's what people needed in order to be inspired and given the confidence to rally around a vision.

The first two years were the hardest. We had a few nights when only one or two students showed up. On several occasions, we had nights when not a single student showed up. Not one. Let's just say that when your job depends on students showing up, you tend not to tell that part of the story very loudly. I would tell students and volunteers that next week would be different, because I did not want them to quit. But I was close to quitting.

At one point, one of the matriarchs of the church pulled me into a side classroom. "I don't know why we hired you," she said. "We don't have any students here. I hope you have a good backup plan, because we don't have the money to pay you very long." No one ever trained me on how to handle that conversation or what to say. I kicked into answer mode, stammering something to the effect that I was confident things would grow in time. On the inside, I was terrified that I had made a big mistake. I could feel the cracks in my soul that were developing under the constant pressure to always be on, be right, and be right on.

By the end of the second year there was a growing sense of God answering our prayers and building momentum. By the end of the fourth year, by the grace of God through the hard work of the volunteers, the interns, and an additional student pastor I was able to hire, we were reaching hundreds of students. But what was strange to me is that even though seemingly everything had changed on the outside, my insides were still responding the same way. I thought the peace I was seeking would be found in being a success, which in my mind meant a lot of people showing up. Now, I had essentially what I wanted to happen, but I didn't have the peace that I thought it would secure for me.

I began to realize that I had become an unintended pretender. I never intended to project more confidence, more certainty, and more answers than I actually had. I never intended to allow my outsides to become bigger than my insides. But increasingly, I could feel the gap between the two.

In the earlier years, the pressure I faced was that no one, or very few people, were showing up and interested. Let's call that a bad pressure. Now the pressure changed. More and more students were interested and showing up. We will call that a good pressure. It was exactly opposite of the pressure of the earlier years, but pressure nonetheless. I would teach and people would tell me how it had helped them. I always would tell them thank you and how glad I was to hear that, but on the inside, I felt a pressure to top that teaching in the next week—more creativity, greater insight, more spiritual oomph. It never occurred to me to ask why I felt those feelings from a simple compliment. We were a success in many respects, but I was dying on the inside. I was soul-exhausted. The pressure to create and sustain momentum was becoming too much for me. Around this time, I remember hearing Bill Hybels reflect on leadership by saying in effect, "The work of God *through* me was killing the work of God *in* me."[2]

I felt like I needed to grow my soul faster to keep up with the demands of the rapidly growing ministry, but it's a funny thing about souls: They do not tend to grow quickly.

Jesus asked a crowd this question: "What good is it for someone to gain the whole world, and yet lose or forfeit their very self?" (Luke 9:25, NIV). Leading—or at least the way I was leading—had become hazardous to my soul. So after a period of prayer and discernment, I resigned.

It sounds noble. It wasn't noble. It was desperate. I needed air.

Though I did not know it at the time, apparently I was not alone. Ministry leadership can be hazardous to your physical and emotional health. The *New York Times* reports:

Members of the clergy now suffer from obesity, hypertension and depression at rates higher than most Americans. In the last decade, their use of antidepressants has risen, while their life expectancy has fallen. Many would change jobs if they could.[3]

Duke University has developed a study that compares ministry leaders with their neighbors in their census tracts. Ministry leaders report significantly higher rates of arthritis, diabetes, high blood pressure, and asthma.[4] Obesity was 10 percent more prevalent in the leadership group.[5] The *New York Times* article sings the virtues of taking time off. However, taking time off without taking time to learn a different way to lead will only lead you to the same place in time.

Working with Yoda: A New Way to Lead

After resigning my position, my wife and I moved to England for five months. We had been invited by a church leader who offered us the chance to simply come and be. That time eventually led to further time out of leadership while I completed my graduate degree at Fuller Theological Seminary in Los Angeles. While in Los Angeles, we were invited by a neighbor to visit a church called Christian Assembly, and we decided to make it our home church for our anticipated two years in Los Angeles. I got involved volunteering, and as it would happen, I was offered a staff position working with twentysomethings.

Although I did not know it at the time, the person who offered me the position turned out to be Yoda. I never knew

Yoda lived in Los Angeles, but he does. His name is Mark Pickerill. I often tell people that Jesus Christ saved my soul from sin. He then sent Mark Pickerill into my life to save my soul from the corrosion of leadership. Without God's work through Mark, I believe the pressures of leading again would have slowly turned me back into an unintended pretender.

After being on staff for about a year, I began to question if our current efforts were the best way to reach young adults in Los Angeles. Good things were happening, but a few of us became curious whether it might be possible to be even more effective in our mission. I wish I could tell you that my time out of leadership and in seminary had taught me new ways of leading under pressure, but the most honest version of the story is I was headed right back into the track of being an unintended pretender. Thankfully, Yoda helped us course correct in his most humble way. Here's how it happened.

We needed space and had been able to purchase additional buildings to repurpose for our efforts. However, the renovation of that building was behind schedule for a fall launch of this new young adult ministry effort. And the logistical challenges were nothing compared to the relational challenges that came with this change: It required a complete shutting down of the two previously existing ministry efforts. If you kill off two ministry efforts that are bad, most people will not care. If you kill off two ministry efforts that are good because you think something better can be arrived at in time, people care a lot more. It's been said that "leaders conduct planned conflict against the status quo."[6] Sometimes the greatest danger to the status quo is simply to ask a different set of open-ended questions.

Prior to accepting the role as the young adult pastor of Christian Assembly, I had been out of leadership for almost two years working on my degree. Unfortunately, put back in the pressure cooker of launching a new ministry, I reverted to the only version of leadership I knew: Be clear, project confidence, pray a lot, and hope it works. If it doesn't, then get your résumé together and hope the next chapter is better than the last one.

Mark knew that we were facing backlashes from a few individuals regarding the changes. He and I were meeting to prepare for a series of upcoming vision nights where I was slated to cast the vision for this new endeavor. In a stroke of genius, Mark wondered aloud, "What if we just tell everyone it's an experiment?" We talked through the positives and negatives of this approach. In that question and the discussion that followed, Mark was leading me to unearth and discover a different way of leadership than I had ever been taught or seen modeled. He was leading me with a question.

Mark's idea was essentially to tell the congregation the most honest version of the story from the beginning. What if we tell them what we think we know and have discovered, but also that we could be wrong and this might be a big failure in the making? What if we just offer all the questions we are wrestling with and invite them to do the same? What if we simply tell them we are curious about whether these changes may lead to more young adults being reached more effectively? What if we ask them to join us in a holy curiosity? One where we are not certain of the answers we will arrive at in time, but where we are confident about the questions we are asking?

Mark helped me find an absolutely new way of thinking about leadership. The most honest version was that we felt we should try something new, we were not certain it was going to work, but we could not shake the feeling that we should give it a shot. We did not have a three-year, five-year, or ten-year strategic plan. We had a mission (to reach young adults in Los Angeles) and a cluster of questions we felt were worth asking.

Prior to launching this new ministry that we called Fusion, we had four vision nights where young adults could come and hear about our thoughts and ask questions. Often we answered their questions with questions back to them—like Jesus often did. During those question-and-answer times, people would ask things such as, "Are you even certain that this is going to work?" It was so freeing to be able to say, "Absolutely not. But some things are worth trying even if the possibility of failure is great." People would ask what the ministry would look like in three years. We were able to tell them the most honest version: "We do not know. Honestly, we are making this up as we go. We are flying the airplane as we build it, and we are looking for you to help us build it with us in ways that we currently can't imagine. This is a big experiment."

I had always thought (and been told) that great leadership is about clarity, certainty, and answers. Instead, Yoda was offering that maybe we can lead better longer with a bit less clarity and less certainty. I was not certain it would work, but I knew that it was truer to actual reality.

In the end, people responded to the most honest version of the story, and our young adult efforts flourished like never before. Reaching young adults in Los Angeles is no easy trick, but something must be working because more than a decade later, we continue to see hundreds and hundreds of young adults in Los Angeles coming to Christ and following him through the efforts that began with a cluster of questions.

The Benefits of Being Question-Led in Our Influence of Others

When you lead from question asking, it unlocks three core benefits for the leader:

It reduces the pressure in the life of the leader. Leading anything—from a family to a small group to a ministry or a local church, among many other things—has enough pressure without adding to it the myth that you know more than you do or are more certain of the future than you actually are. If you launch a new endeavor as the answer-person, then you had better be prepared to always have the answers. The way you launch something is the way you had better be prepared to lead it. It's been said that the way you win people is the way you keep people. If you win them with having all the answers, then you will slowly lose them the moment it becomes clear that you don't have all the answers or your answers aren't delivering the promised results in their lives. With the number of leaders who crumple under pressure in any field, whenever we can reduce pressure, that's a very good thing.

It increases the humility in the soul of the leader. To stand before a group of people that you are hoping to mobilize toward a goal, and admit the limits of your confidence and knowledge, is a humbling position to be in—which is another way of saying, it's a very good position to be in. The Scriptures tell us that the humble will see their God at work and be glad, that God cares for the humble but keeps his distance from the proud, and that God opposes the proud but gives grace to the humble (Psalms 69:32; 138:6; Proverbs 3:34).

We had a mission (to reach and make disciples of young adults in Los Angeles) that we felt was important. Our explicit invitation to the young adults gathered was not to be a cog in a predetermined set of answers that we had envisioned without their input; instead, the invitation was to join us on a mission where we knew that reaching young adults was important but we would have to learn together how to do it. Once the dust settled, we had a cadre of young adults who wanted in on the mission.

Our questions began with whether the gospel had lost its touch with young adults in Los Angeles. And if so, why? And if not, why were young adults underrepresented in local churches in Los Angeles? Our explicit invitation to explore these questions with us was intended to stoke a holy curiosity that would move us to live into answers, not just talk about them.

Slowly, the questions evolved into clumps that we saw as three directions. The first clump centered on upward questions, such as "How do young adults connect to God? What can we do to create spaces and relationships to encourage that?" The second clump centered on inward questions, such as whether young adults felt the need for community and if so, how we could create relational communities centered on Christ. The third clump centered on what we deemed the outward questions—biblical justice and sharing the good news of Jesus with young adults. What are the most effective ways to encourage the cultivation of a community of biblical justice, coupled with doing these things in Jesus' name? When a young adult does come to a first-time belief in Christ, how do you actually make a disciple of them in modern-day Los Angeles with all its mobility and transience?

The point here is that we had a mission and lots of questions without any clear answers. Ours was a heuristic process that involved a lot of trial and error as we together looked to live into the discovery of some solutions.

One of the things that can derail a leader is the slow slide to arrogance, thinking like Peter once did that even if everyone else failed, somehow we will not. We might have an exceptional track record, but no one except the Lord can guarantee with integrity anything about the future.

It keeps the leader in the position of a learner first, a leader second. We are now more than a decade into our current iteration of Fusion, our experiment of the mission of reaching young adults. When I started that effort, I was a twentysomething. In that sense, I was within the generation that I was on a mission to impact. A decade later, of course, that's not the case. The time has only shown me even more the importance of constantly asking open-ended questions around the mission to a new group of young adults. The further I am removed in age from this age group, the more imperative it's become for me to keep curiously asking questions to those who are within the age group and want to try to live into the answers for their peers. This is the beauty of question-led leadership. It allows for constant adaptation, evolution, and organic changes that match the very mission you are on together.

The first part of the call of Jesus to his disciples was to come and be with him. We begin as learners. Jesus' call also included the fact that he will make us fishers of people. The moment he does that, those people will begin to look to us for leadership. As that happens, we now have the dual responsibility to be a learner *and* a leader.

The subtle temptation is to become a leader first, and then a learner second. Once that happens, the temptation is to stop learning altogether. No one intends for that to happen, but the limited amount of time coupled with the increasing pressures of leadership can make that our unintended reality.

I can tell when I am sliding into leading without learning when most of what I talk about in my relationship with Christ or in what I am discovering from the questions I am asking are all from long ago rather than something recent, fresh, and current. The best leaders are leaders who are learning first and leading second; their leadership will constantly be informed and updated by the many experiments that are being lived out from the questions that are being asked. The leaders who learn first are ones who are asking of themselves and the Lord first before they begin to ask the questions of others. They then also listen to what is happening in the lives of those who are living into effective answers, and then share those learnings not as a decree, but instead to set the stage for asking why these things seem to be working within this context.

The benefits of question-led leadership are not limited to the life of a leader. The decision of a leader to tell the most honest version of your story, coupled with leading from questions rather than only answers, also has a profound effect on those you are serving. Even if you would never consider yourself a leader, you are impacted from the benefits of being led by a person who lives from the power of asking the right questions. We will dig into that in the next chapter.

Jesus' Questions for a Recovering Unintended Pretender

Is there any hope for those of us who feel like we've become an unintended pretender? Thankfully, there is.

Peter claimed that he would not abandon Jesus even if everyone else did. He claimed that he would not cave to the pressure even if everyone else did. However, when the chips were down and the pressure was up, Peter lied three times in his denials of Jesus. There is nothing in his story from the day he left his fishing nets to follow Jesus that indicated he intended to be a fraud. He never intended to oversell and under-deliver. Peter learned something about himself. But he's also about to learn something about Jesus, too.

After Jesus is crucified and is resurrected from the dead, one of the first things he does is to go looking for Peter, his follower-become-leader-become-unintended pretender. Jesus finds Peter with some of the other disciples fishing on the Sea of Galilee (see John 21:1-17).

Jesus, Peter, and the other disciples share a meal of cooked fish and some bread. As is often his pattern, Jesus leads with a question: "Simon son of John, do you love me more than these?"

The word that is translated *love* here is the Greek word *agape*. It carries with it a sense of unconditional love. In effect, Jesus is saying, "Remember when you said your devotion to me was greater than anyone else's? Do you still think that?"

Prior to his denials, Simon Peter would have declared, "Yes! I *agape* you more than these other disciples!" But now, Simon Peter answers with the most honest version of his story: "Yes, Lord, you know that I *phileo* you." Peter's answer does not compare his love to the others (as his declaration had earlier). And notice he uses a different word than Jesus used. *Phileo* is a form of love, but it is a different form of love than *agape*.[7] It is the love between close friends, but not necessarily unconditional.[8] Simon is choosing a lesser, more humble and restricted version of the word *love*. Simon had made his declaration that he would never deny Jesus in the midst of an argument over who was the greatest disciple. Now, on the other side of reality—that he could not deliver on his promise—Peter chooses to acknowledge the most honest version of his love. It's a kind of love, but it's neither unlimited nor unconditional.

Again Jesus said, "Simon son of John, do you *agape* me?" Again Simon Peter responds with, "Yes, Lord, you know that I *phileo* you." Jesus is leading Peter by asking him this question. In effect, Jesus is seeing what Peter has learned about himself and what version of his story he is willing to tell.

The third time, Jesus changes his question to Peter: "Do you *phileis* me?" Jesus now switches to the same word that Peter has used twice in a row.[9] Peter is saddened, though not just at being asked the same question three times (paralleling his three denials of Jesus). He is coming to terms with the limitations of his love and the most honest version of his story.

The most honest version of our story is never as glamorous as our more edited versions. You can almost feel Peter's dejection and disappointment with the truest version of who he is at this point. All his confidence and self-assertion have failed him. He hasn't measured up. Have you ever felt that way? That your best ended up being short of what you pledged? Who hasn't? Ironically, our least honest versions usually give glory to ourselves and rob it from God, while our most honest versions, with all our limitations and failures included, are the ones that allow the power of God's grace to shine most brightly.

Peter's answer the third time begins with the affirmation that Jesus knows everything. The recent events of Peter's life have proven that when Jesus asks us questions, it's not because he doesn't know the answer; it's usually because we don't know the answer and he is leading us to it. Jesus knew the most honest version of Peter's leadership even when Peter was still naive.

With leadership philosophies, as well as ninth-grade friendships, sometimes the best things come from your worst moments. Each time Peter tells Jesus "I *phileo* you," Jesus commissions Peter to feed his sheep. In effect Jesus is saying, "Continue to lead, but lead from the most honest version of your story. It will be better for you as a leader. It will also be better for those you lead."

Questions Worth Being Curious About

1. Have you ever given in to the pressure to pretend that you know more than you do? In your case, why did that happen? What does it show you about yourself?

2. Is there anyone in your life who knows the most honest version of your story? If not, how can you move toward having at least one person who knows your most honest story?

3. If you are a leader or influencer of others, do you ever feel the pressure to know more answers than you actually know? How do you respond in those moments? Why do you respond that way?

4. Whether you are a leader or not, if you adopted a more question-led approach to your interactions with others, how would that help you?

3

A COMMUNITY OF CO-CONSPIRATORS: HOW QUESTIONS SPARK AND SUSTAIN MOMENTUM IN PEOPLE

It is not the answer that enlightens, but the question.

DECOUVERTES

How many loaves do you have?

JESUS, IN MATTHEW 15:34 (NIV)

GREG MACDONALD IS ONE OF MY HEROES.

Greg and I became friends not too long after I moved to Los Angeles. He was a twentysomething who had come to Christ several years earlier. An engineer by trade, having done everything from dismantling chemical weapons to building theme parks, he is literally building the Magic Kingdom for Disney.

One day about a decade ago, Greg came to me feeling a bit unsettled with his life group. He had been serving as life group leader, but it felt stale and stagnant to him. He was curious if I might have an answer about how to put some zest back into the group.

I knew I could offer a few tweaks that might prolong the

group for a couple of months, but I genuinely did not have a magic bullet to offer. But Greg eventually landed on a single question that he wanted to explore with his life group: "What does God say in the Bible about the poor?"

When Greg announced the change in format, he lost some group members. That's fairly normal. Not all the people will embrace all the change all the time. Greg decided to stick with it for six months, and he set out to answer that question with those who continued in the group. They started in the Old Testament and made it all the way through the end of the New Testament, focusing only on passages that had something to say about the poor.

At the end of that study, Greg's questions changed from "What does God say about the poor?" to "What is God asking of us now that we know what God says about the poor?" Greg's initial question was leading him and his group to try to live into an answer. What has happened since then still amazes me to this day. We will come back to that later.

The Other Cost of Unintended Pretenders

Good people can become unintended pretenders by virtue of the pressures of leadership. But the effects do not end there. The ripple effects of leaders who pretend that we know more than we do, are more confident than we are, and have more solutions than we rightfully do, extend out to those we serve. When leaders pretend, we end up disempowering the next wave of people whom God might be inviting to lead or serve in some way. We may conclude we are not cut out to lead simply because we cannot imagine leading with such absolute confidence and answers to all or even most of the questions. Many leaders are the "walking wounded," but their followers are often the "sitting silent."

The dirty little secret, the most honest version of the leadership story, is that we do not often have as much confidence as we project or as many answers as we let people believe we have. It's not a malicious choice, but left unchecked, our unintended pretending becomes the unintended disempowering of another's life.

There is some good news to be found here. If we leaders are ruthless with ourselves, snuffing out the places where we project more answers, knowledge, and confidence than we actually have, we can clear the way for others to believe that maybe God can use them, too. If we couple that with asking those we serve simple questions and letting them discover the answers (rather than giving them our answers), we can empower the next wave of leaders. We might seem a bit less impressive to those we lead, but it's that very thing that empowers them to get involved. In the Kingdom of God, everyone gets to play because everyone has a part to play.

Staring at the Ocean with a Bucket

Eventually, Greg prayerfully decided to try to do something about the homeless within Los Angeles. They, he reasoned, were the poor within his reach.

He might as well have decided to try to empty the ocean with a bucket. Most people know Los Angeles is a big city—the second largest in the United States—but they do not have a sense of just how big. More people live in greater Los Angeles than live in forty-three American states.[1] When Los Angeles has a problem, it tends to be a big one, simply due to the scale.

Homelessness in Los Angeles is a big problem. New York City and Los Angeles jockey for position for the dubious distinction of which city has the most homeless people at any given time, but the number is equivalent to a small town: just under 58,000 people.[2] There is a fifty-block area east of downtown Los Angeles that is locally known as "Skid Row." Cardboard boxes, tents, and shopping carts mix with the smell of urine on the streets. It's not a pleasant scene. Not somewhere most people choose to spend their time.

Homelessness is not just a big problem; it's also complex, and complex problems usually do not get resolved with simple answers. The issues confronting the people who are homeless in Los Angeles are usually more than simply not having a job or a place to stay. Roughly one-third of the homeless people in Los Angeles are mentally ill, roughly a third are addicts of some sort, and roughly one-fifth have a physical disability.[3] It is the kind of reality that can paralyze even the most well-intentioned people who want to make a difference in Jesus' name.

Greg is a smart guy. He was well versed in many of the questions that cluster around the issue of homelessness. For example, how do the decisions of the insurance and mental health industries drive how many mentally ill are on the streets? What responsibility does the government have in light of the taxes collected to care for these people? Apart from systematic questions, there are also questions of how individual decisions and individual responsibilities affect homelessness. Even further, there are questions about why homelessness continues to be a problem in light of the resources that are available to people, ranging from shelters to rehab centers, job training programs, and more.

Homelessness is the kind of problem that is so overwhelming, with so many competing views on how to best address it, that many people simply do nothing.

And yet, homelessness in Los Angeles is not the first overwhelming problem that followers of Jesus have been confronted with. In fact, it happened in the pages of the Bible.

How Much Bread Do You Have?

Jesus was by the Sea of Galilee when a crowd gathered to hear him teach and for the sick to be healed. We pick up the story there:

> Then Jesus called his disciples and told them, "I feel sorry for these people. They have been here with me for three days, and they have nothing left to eat. I don't want to send them away hungry, or they will faint along the way."

> The disciples replied, "Where would we
> get enough food here in the wilderness for such
> a huge crowd?"
>
> MATTHEW 15:32-33

Jesus does what Jesus often does with questions. He answers it with a question: "How much bread do you have?" (verse 34).

There was another time, further back in the story of God and his people, when the people did not have any bread. God had delivered the Israelites from slavery in Egypt. They left Egypt in a large crowd, even larger than the one that gathered with Jesus on this day. Then the people of God were sustained by manna—in essence, food from heaven. As Jews, the disciples would have known that story by heart, probably hearing it their whole lives. In fact, the Israelites were so concerned about remembering that story of God's provision that they collected a jar of manna and placed it in the Ark of the Covenant.

Among other things, the Ark of the Covenant functioned as the container of things that God wanted his people to remember, things they wanted to remember about their interactions with God. The Ark was basically a time capsule of remembrance, one generation saying to future generations, "Don't forget! These stories actually happened. We actually would have died without that manna as our daily bread."

Fast-forward to Jesus in the wilderness with a large crowd of people. This episode of Jesus' leadership is near the end of several interactions Jesus has with his followers about bread (see Matthew 14–16). Sometimes the bread is actual bread; other times *bread* is a metaphor for something else. In one instance the disciples are confronted with an overwhelmingly large, hungry crowd.[4] They watch Jesus take five loaves and two fish, look up toward heaven, and bless them. Then, breaking the loaves into pieces, he gives the bread to the disciples, who distribute it to the people. It seems Jesus is interested in doing something *in* his followers, and then doing something *through* his followers.

Then there is a discussion about whether a person can be unacceptable because of the food they eat. Immediately following that is a discussion whether you should give "food" (used here metaphorically) to those it was not intended for. After that, the feeding of four thousand, where Jesus asks the disciples, "How much bread do you have?" And finally, after that, there is a conversation about the "yeast of the Pharisees," in which the disciples think Jesus is upset because they have not brought any bread for their trip.

Jesus connects all these events by a series of questions:

You have so little faith! Why are you arguing with each other about having no bread? Don't you understand even yet? Don't you remember the 5,000 I fed with five loaves, and the baskets of leftovers you picked up? Or the 4,000 I fed with seven loaves, and the large baskets of leftovers you picked up?

MATTHEW 16:8-10[5]

The feeding of the five thousand is not some distant memory. Can't you just picture it? As the disciples are picking up the baskets of leftover food, they have to be thinking, *What just happened?* As Jews, the story they have heard their whole lives about God providing bread from heaven just happened in their life, in their story.

How Much Bread Do You Have?

Jesus asked questions all the time of those who were following him. But it's not just that he asks his followers questions. It's the nature of the questions and how he leads them through those questions. In this case, his question is an invitation to get involved, to be part of what happens next. Ultimately, Jesus is interested not only in people who cheer from the sidelines; he's looking for a community of people who will get in the game. Jesus could have told the disciples, "Remember the manna from heaven from the book of Exodus? Well, sit back and watch it happen again." Instead he says, essentially, "How can you be involved in this situation?" Jesus is not just interested in getting the job done; he's interested in getting his community involved to get the job done. He's not just interested in filling the crowd's stomachs; he's interested in transforming his disciples' hearts.

By asking "How much bread do you have?" Jesus is moving his disciples from the sidelines to play their part, however small it might be. He is creating a community of people who become co-conspirators with him to do something about the hunger of the world. They are invited to be involved, not simply watch from the sidelines.

Nevertheless, with this invitation Jesus' disciples find themselves staring down an impossible task with few resources. Sound familiar? Most people I know see needs that far surpass the resources within their grasp. We all want a bit more time, a few more people to volunteer, and a couple more loaves of bread. Then we'd be able to do something about the hungry masses.

But this story of feeding the four thousand is not just about God's provision. It's also about *how* God wants to provide for the overwhelming needs of the crowd. The disciples are central to all of this. Jesus is inviting them to become world changers by the profound act of trusting him with the resources they had. He is asking them to become part of something larger than their own stomachs. Jesus doesn't ask the *crowd* how many loaves they have; he asks the disciples.

That question would dredge up all sorts of fears of inadequacy, greed, and entitlement. They'd probably think things like *I don't see how my little loaf will make much of a difference in the face of overwhelming needs.* Or *If I give Jesus my loaf, am I going to end up hungry?* Or *Shouldn't these people have planned better?* Of course, I don't know that the disciples thought these things, but I know I have.

The feeding of the four thousand is a story of God providing for people, but it's also the story of a leader who could have done it all by himself but chose instead to ask a question that invited others to be involved. Jesus could have just asked for manna to rain down from heaven, but instead, he wants those who follow him to be involved in this miracle. And he gets them involved by asking them a question.

Skid Row, a Few Egg McMuffins, and a Prayer

Two thousand years after the feeding of the four thousand, my friend Greg MacDonald was faced with his own over-whelmingly large crowd of hungry people: the homeless in Los Angeles. His life group had become convinced from the Scriptures that God has a heart for the poor, and that fol-lowers of Jesus have a responsibility to the poor. Greg also knew that there were all sorts of questions about the "best" way to alleviate homelessness. Refusing to be paralyzed by the overwhelming nature of the problem or the sheer num-ber of questions that surround homelessness, Greg centered on a single question: What is God asking me to do to care and show compassion to these poor people in our city? Greg didn't try to answer every question about homelessness, just this one.

Here's what happened next. Greg and a few others decided to begin to make regular Sunday morning trips to Skid Row. With no fanfare, they would meet early each Sunday morn-ing. They would pray together, and then, with whatever money they were able to gather up from among their little group, they would purchase a few Egg McMuffins from the local McDonalds on the way down to Skid Row. I remember going with them on a few of the initial trips as we simply built relationships with a few people. There was no grand plan to solve all the complex problems that contributed to homelessness. Just the question Jesus asked the original disciples: "How much bread do you have?" Greg's answer varied each week from between four to ten Egg McMuffins.

Two critics arose from outside our church; they came to me arguing that Greg and his group were doing more harm than good. Our church, they contended, was exacerbating the problem and prolonging people's homelessness by offering them free food. It should be noted that such arguments usually come from people who have never been homeless. I have yet to meet a person who decided to stay homeless to get a free Egg McMuffin once a week. Egg McMuffins are good, but not *that* good.

Nevertheless, the critics led Greg to revisit questions of homelessness specifically in light of Jesus' teachings. Are we doing more harm than good? We understand the issues are complex, but how do we keep that complexity from lulling us into doing nothing? We thought of Jesus' parable of the Good Samaritan. The Samaritan did not—maybe could not—solve all the social and systematic issues that led to thieves preying on people and a man being beaten on the side of the road. The Samaritan simply loved his neighbor by doing what he could do, not by doing nothing because he could not do everything.

Greg was faithful with his Sunday visits to Skid Row

for many years. What had started as a few people slowly grew to a dozen or more. A handful of Egg McMuffins now became a couple dozen. People living on Skid Row moved from being strangers to acquaintances to friends. Whenever possible, the good news of Jesus was shared with these new friends. Questions about homelessness became less philosophical and more personal; "the homeless" were no longer just a class of people who are poor, but individuals with names and stories. The answers to those questions are never exactly the same, because each person is different, but they include such things as job training programs and substance recovery programs. Greg and his friends discovered that in some cases substance abuse was covering up grief—from the loss of a loved one or other such things. We moved from asking "What is God asking us to do to love and serve the local poor?" to "What is God asking us to do to love and serve Felipe, Anita, and Richard?"

I had wanted our church to engage the issues of the city, but I never had a vision for a homeless ministry per se. That was all God's work through Greg MacDonald and the others who were asking the right kind of questions that empowered them to live into answers of love and service in Jesus' name.

Benefits to Followers of a Question-Led Leader

The right kind of question holds the power to unlock new ways of living as God helps us to live into the answer. We first have to give up our addiction to always having an answer and sometimes simply be humble enough to ask a question. However, questions that humble us do not always move us. Having been humbled by some questions, we need to be empowered by others that help us move from mere humility to humble action. Our action is not based on believing we know everything or even most things, but rather that we trust God to lead us to live into the answer of the question he's placed on our heart.

Greg was not just asking questions for himself, he was asking others those same questions, inviting them to develop answers, to get involved in tangible ways, and to live out answers in everyday ways together. When we share our questions with others, it's remarkable what can happen. It's true that some people will lose interest and walk away, maybe because the questions are too overwhelming, or because they prefer inaction to imperfect action. That happened to Jesus, too. We must not let ourselves become too discouraged by people walking away. Greater things will arise from those of us who stick around seeking to try to live into the answers of the questions that are being asked.

Three benefits accrue to a group of people led by questions:

Questions unleash greater creativity for the future. When a leader seems to have all the answers, then the leader's vision—and the ways that vision is lived out—tends to be limited to the creativity of one person (or a small group). However, when a leader asks the right questions to those who are within their community and invites them to discover the answers together, people will often not only create more, but do so more creatively. It's not simply that they do more (though they often do); it's also that they do it in ways that the original person might not have ever envisioned. Now, this is not the case for Jesus, who already knew the best and most creative (literally, as he prayed and more bread was created) way to handle the hungry crowd of four thousand. However, for those of us who are not named Jesus, greater creativity will be unleashed in the communities we serve when we invite ideas from the people around us. The creativity of all of us is greater than the creativity of only one of us.

Just because an idea is creative does not mean it's the best idea to attempt. Part of the role of the leader is to discern which ideas that arise from the community are the best options to pursue together. However, when a leader asks the right questions of those who follow them, it gives the opportunity for the inherent creativity within the community of people to emerge. From there, it gives the opportunity for the best of the creative ideas to actually be attempted. Often, that idea may be one that the leader would have never thought of trying.

Questions unleash greater passion in people. When a leader slides into being the answer person, the passion for the vision and the task of recruiting people, resources, and time toward that vision falls almost wholly to the leader. However, when a leader recenters his or her efforts on asking the right kinds of questions, then those who begin to find answers to those questions inherently own the vision in a greater way. People tend to prefer supporting an answer they created or discovered over one that was prepackaged and handed to them. Adult learning theory confirms this, telling us that most adults learn best from "approaches to learning that are problem-based and collaborative rather than didactic, and also emphasizes more equality between the teacher and learner."[6] Using questions to teach and lead adults helps them to not only own the vision, but to invite others to join them in their vision. This leads to the replication of leadership, as people engage others with the same questions that were asked of them.

Recruiting people to a mission is part of the job of any leader. The key is how we do it. If we recruit people only by giving them a sales pitch, then we will have to constantly resell them on our predetermined plan. However, if we recruit people by guiding them on a self-discovery process of what God is inviting *them* to do, they tend to have much greater endurance in that effort. Our culture tends to use the word *passion* as meaning being emotionally excited. However, the first definition of *passion* is suffering. So when I say that questions unleash greater passion, I mean that people are more willing to suffer for, sacrifice for, and endure for an answer they discovered than for one that someone else handed to them.

It's a slower process to get people involved in this way, because it requires more front-end work on their part, but it's also a better process of keeping people involved, because their endurance comes from their own convictions, not convictions simply borrowed from the leader. Borrowed convictions don't endure very long in a world full of challenges. Borrowed passions tend to be fickle.

Questions unleash greater faith-building memories for people. Too often people within a local church can live on vicarious memories that are told within their community. These stories are good, necessary, and inspiring. But they are not nearly as powerful as when the story is your own story. Vicarious memories tend to create vicarious faith. Personal memories tend to create personal faith. The disciples had always heard and known the old stories of God providing for his people in the wilderness when they were delivered from Egypt; now they had their own story of God working in their own generation.

Jesus asks his followers how many loaves they have, but then later he asks them a different question: "Don't you remember the 4,000 I fed with seven loaves, and the large basket of leftovers you picked up?" Here the challenge he gives them is to remember their own stories of God working in their lives. When people get involved and God does something, they no longer need to live on the vicarious faith of the leader or the leader's story. Now they can remember from their own lives when they were involved about how God used them.

Fifty Thousand Egg McMuffins and Counting

Faced with a large, hungry crowd, Jesus asked the original disciples, "How much bread to do you have?"

"Seven loaves and a few fish," they responded.

Jesus took the loaves and fish, prayed, broke the bread, and gave it back to the disciples who distributed it to the crowd. Everyone had enough to eat, with baskets left over.

Greg was faced with his own large, hungry crowd in Los Angeles. You can just feel Jesus asking him the same question: "Greg, how much bread do you have?"

"About four Egg McMuffins," Greg would have responded.

Let's fast-forward about ten years to present day. Along the way, Greg's job was transferred to another part of the world. Others asked what was going to happen to the homeless effort once it became known Greg would be moving. I didn't have any answers for them, but often God unleashes his power in ordinary people when they realize that it's either them or no one. God gives power to those who are willing to live out an answer.

In this instance, others stepped up. A handful of people each Sunday morning grew to a network of about fifty people serving about one hundred meals on a given morning. They have switched over the years from Egg McMuffins to a variety of other meals. They go every single weekend, including and especially holidays. I do not know how long the effort will last, but I do know that each life touched through it while it lasts matters. What they do is not fancy. It's not spectacular. As Jud Wilhite once said, "God didn't call us to be spectacular. He called us to be faithful."[7]

By my count, what started with a question, a small group

of disciples, and four Egg McMuffins, has now become almost 50,000 meals shared in Jesus' name over the last decade. My friend Greg worked at building the Magic Kingdom for his day job, but sometimes it seems like Disney is not the only kingdom that has some magic to it.

Questions Worth Being Curious About

1. If you are a follower of Jesus, what question are you most compelled to try to live into at this point in your life?

2. When you face a large social problem (such as home-lessness), what is your response? Do you feel that you can't do anything until you answer all the questions that surround that issue? If so, why is that?

3. Can you think of a time when God used you to make a difference in another person's life? How did that happen? How did you feel as that happened? What obstacles did you encounter, either in your own heart or outside of you?

4. If you are a leader, are you quick to provide answers to those you serve? Why is that? What would be lost if you stopped doing that? What would be gained if you inserted prayerful questions where you previously felt compelled to provide an answer?

ASKING OUR WAY TO THE WORLD GOD WANTS

PART 2

4

THE FOUNDATIONAL QUESTION: WHAT IS THE GOSPEL OF JESUS?

Then who in the world can be saved?
JESUS' DISCIPLES, IN MARK 10:26

Is anything worth more than your soul?
JESUS, IN MATTHEW 16:26

CAN YOU THINK OF A MOMENT when you experienced good news that brought great joy into your life?

For me, one memorable experience happened during the summer between my freshman and sophomore years in college. My friend Mike and I decided to spend the summer backpacking in the American West. As part of that, we planned out a route that included hiking a couple of weeks in the backcountry of Yellowstone National Park. We mapped out a route that would keep us far from roads for close to two weeks.

When you are backpacking a long distance, the lighter you pack the better. So we meticulously planned our food for the exact number of days that we expected to be on the trail. We were gourmet backpackers, so mostly our food consisted of Pop-Tarts and peanut butter and jelly sandwiches.

The morning of the last day we started out on a fifteen-mile hike with blistered feet, sore muscles, and a steady drizzle of rain. We were tired, but we knew the promised land of Grant Village was awaiting us at the end of the day. Grant Village offered the glory of hot showers, a buffet of food, and the chance to sleep in a lodge.

A fifteen-mile hike seems manageable to two twenty-year-olds when you are sitting in a coffee shop mapping it out. It seems less manageable hobbling on blistered feet at the end of two weeks of backpacking. It was past lunch when we each ate our last sandwich and any other bits of food we had left. The rain worsened, making the hiking slow going, and we were facing the prospect of hiking into the night to make it to Grant Village.

We thought it could not get any worse. It did.

About eight trail miles from Grant Village, we saw something in the distance that we had never seen before on our trip: ribbons strung back and forth across the trail from tree to tree. As we got closer, we saw that it was not ribbon but caution tape, strung high and low across the trail for a distance of about twenty-five yards—one big three-dimensional spiderweb of caution.

Then we saw a sign nailed to a tree: "Caution! Intense grizzly bear activity ahead. Turn around. Do not use this trail."

"Turn around. Do not use this trail" are not the words you want to see when you are cold, wet, sore, and out of peanut butter and jelly sandwiches. To say it was bad news is an understatement.

Exhaustion, coupled with hunger, is the playground for bad decision-making. I vividly remember Mike and me having a conversation about just how intense this grizzly bear activity really was. Could it really be that bad? Maybe they were exaggerating a bit. Plus, to turn around meant making our fifteen-mile day much longer, and it was already moving toward evening. We literally almost walked into intense grizzly bear activity because we could not face the prospect of another day on the trail without a peanut butter and jelly sandwich.

Cooler heads prevailed, though, and we backtracked a number of miles to a side trail that eventually led us to a road. It was now evening and still raining, we had no food, and Grant Village was still about ten more miles up the road. Too exhausted and blistered to keep going, we decided to try hitchhiking. Maybe some good soul would have mercy on us.

There were not many cars on this dark, unlit road, but the ones that did come along just kept driving. I can't say I blame them. Picking up two rough-looking twenty-year-old men on the side of an unlit road in the middle of the wilderness is usually not on most people's agendas. But then, amazingly, a car pulled over. We grabbed our bags and hobbled up to the driver's window.

The driver rolled down her window just enough to make a small opening. She lifted her lips toward the opening and asked us a single question: "If I let you in the car, you're not going to kill me, are you?" I am not making this up. She actually asked us that question. I have often wondered why. Maybe she thought murderers hold a high regard for honesty.

We assured her that we were not planning on killing her, but that we wanted to get to Grant Village, the promised land of hot food, warm showers, and a dry lodge. She also was headed to Grant Village and agreed to take us with her. We climbed into her backseat with all of our baggage.

That dark, rainy evening, a woman took us where we wanted to go but were unable to get to on our own. She was news that brought us joy that night. It was not just great news that we believed; it was great news that we experienced.

I don't remember her name, but in my mind I have named her Grace.

Would I Like It If Jesus Turned Out to Be the Lord?

The woman who pulled over on the side of road did not give Mike and me advice on how to get to Grant Village. She *happened* to us. She made the choice to get involved when others passed by. She invited us to respond by climbing in her car, even with all of our baggage. All we could do was rejoice and jump in the car.

Dallas Willard finds questions a helpful point of entry for some people to understand the gospel.

> Often a good starting point when trying to help those who do not believe in God or accept Christ as Lord is to get them to deal honestly with the question: Would I *like* for there to be a God? Or, would I *like* it if Jesus turned out to be Lord? This may help them realize the extent to which what they *want* to be the case is controlling their ability to see what *is* the case.[1]

Not only does Willard give us a way forward in leading people, but his suggestion centers on helping those who do not believe in God or accept Christ through the power of the right questions. For those who follow Jesus, the gospel is the history and story that we tell. It is also the truth that we experience. The word in the Greek for the gospel (*euaggelio*) literally translated means "the news that brings joy." For those who lead others to follow Jesus, "What is the gospel?" is a cornerstone question. We must be careful that we don't answer it by turning the gospel into a to-do list. As David Martyn Lloyd-Jones noted:

> The Gospel is good news, not good advice. . . .
> Advice is counsel about something to do and it hasn't happened yet, but you can do it. News is a report

about something that has happened—you can't do anything about it—it's been done for you and all you can do is respond to it.[2]

When Jesus began his public ministry, the news that brings great joy that he declared was so decisive that it required a decision on the part of those who heard it. He proclaimed, "The time is fulfilled, and the kingdom of God is at hand; repent and believe in the gospel" (Mark 1:15, ESV). The word he used translated "gospel" was not simply a religious word in his day; it was a term used in the secular world of his day in the Roman Empire to announce the rise of a new king or a victory in battle. For example, one well-known historic Roman inscription from that time starts with "The beginning of the gospel of Caesar Augustus."[3] Jesus is declaring the rise of the Kingdom of God as good news for all people everywhere to take notice of and to respond. Dallas Willard observed, "The Gospel means that this universe is a perfectly safe place for you to be."[4] The gospel of Jesus Christ is such a majestic occurrence that even the angels long to look into these things (see 1 Peter 1:12).

The Problem with Half of the Gospel

God loves us, even in our sin (see Romans 5:8). But God's affection toward us is only part of the story. Being embraced by God is only half of the gospel. Transformation is the other half. Both halves of the gospel must be understood and experienced to live the lives we were created to live. Leighton Ford has summarized the gospel of Jesus this way: "God loves us as we are, but too much to leave us that way." Dallas Willard defined love as the *"will to good"* for another.[5] God's love is active. He sent his Son Jesus Christ so that we did not have to live forever in our sin, suffering its effects on us, our relationship with God, and one another.

When people receive only half of a gospel, you can tell by how they respond. One of the great stories of a gospel gone sideways is the story of the English Duke of Wellington facing the French commander Napoleon in a great battle. The future of England was in great uncertainty. A sailing ship signaled with code flags to convey the news of the outcome to another signalman at the top of Winchester Cathedral. The first word was signaled in: *Wellington*. The second word was signaled in: *Defeated*. Then a fog came down and the ship could no longer be seen. "Wellington defeated" was the news that was spread across all of England. There was great gloom. But then the fog lifted about three hours later, and the signal came again, this time with two words that were lost from the first message: "Wellington Defeated the Enemy." Once the people had gotten the true news, their response radically changed from gloom to rejoicing. All across England you could tell which version of the news people had heard based on how they responded and how they were living.

If you don't understand the news, or only receive half of the message, then your response won't match what has actually happened. In other words, *the version of the gospel you accept will determine the pathway of discipleship you walk.*

So then, the gospel happens *to* us, but then it must also happen *in* us. We are loved before we make any changes. But we are loved also so that we are empowered to make changes. God desires to change us not because he wants to love us, but because he already does love us. A person who desires to help others know and live out the implications of the gospel, therefore, must first embrace the whole gospel for himself. It is hard to lead people to places that you have never been.

A Tale of Three Cities

Embracing and living by both halves of the gospel has been an ongoing leadership challenge in the community of Jesus. One of the great leaders of the early church, the apostle Paul, had to address the effect of understanding only half of the gospel among the communities of Jesus in Corinth and Galatia.

Corinth was known in the first-century Roman world, among other things, as a city of sexuality. So when the gospel arrived in Corinth, the tendency was to adopt only the first half of the gospel: God loves us as we are. This became such a focal point that God's grace and love for us became an excuse to sin even more. Some people began to justify increasingly outrageous sexual behaviors on the basis that God loves us, and therefore we can do what we want.

Paul writes, "I can hardly believe the report about the

sexual immorality going on among you—something that even pagans don't do. I am told that a man in your church is living in sin with his stepmother. You are so proud of yourselves" (1 Corinthians 5:1-2). Why would they be proud? Because they thought they were "allowed to do anything" (1 Corinthians 6:12). Understanding only the first half of the gospel often misunderstands the gospel as a license to sin.

While some in Corinth focused on living only the first half of the gospel, others in the church in the city of Galatia were focused on living only the second half of the gospel: God loves us too much to leave us as we are. They did this by teaching that Gentile believers needed to obey the Old Testament law of circumcision and observe certain special holidays. In effect, God's love had to be earned through actions. Paul refutes that understanding of the gospel: "You are following a different way that pretends to be the Good News but is not the Good News at all" (Galatians 1:6-7). As a leader, Paul continues with strong words, "Let God's curse fall on anyone, including us or even an angel from heaven, who preaches a different kind of Good News than the one we preached to you" (verse 8). He is underlining the fact that leaders must be certain we are teaching the whole gospel.

It is no small thing to live by half of the gospel. Paul says to them, "I fear for you" (Galatians 4:11). Understanding only the second half of the gospel misinterprets it as a rigid, fear-based legalism.

There is a third city where Paul engages the two halves

of the gospel. It's here that Paul most succinctly helps us see that the gospel contains both halves working together or it is not good news at all. To the church in Ephesus, Paul declares the good news that "God is so rich in mercy, and he loved us so much, that even though we were dead because of our sins, he gave us life when he raised Christ from the dead. (It is only by God's grace that you have been saved!)" (Ephesians 2:4-5).

We see here that the gospel is news of what God has done, not advice for self-improvement. But Paul continues in one seamless declaration of the whole news that brings great joy:

> God saved you by his grace when you believed. And you can't take credit for this; it is a gift from God. Salvation is not a reward for the good things we have done, so none of us can boast about it. For we are God's masterpiece. He has created us anew in Christ Jesus, so we can do the good things he planned for us long ago.
>
> EPHESIANS 2:8-10

The gospel is about what God has done, and the news of what God has done has the power to change everything. We find ourselves damaged by evil, knowing intuitively that we were created for good. It is in Jesus Christ that we are restored for better and then sent to heal others by doing the good things God planned for us in advance.[6] N. T. Wright summarizes the gospel of Jesus this way:

> The gospel is the royal announcement that the crucified and risen Jesus, who died for our sins and rose again according to the Scriptures, has been enthroned as the true Lord of the world. When this gospel is preached, God calls people to salvation, out of sheer grace, leading them to repentance and faith in Jesus Christ as the risen Lord.[7]

The gospel is not just the thing that saves us; it's also the thing that matures us. Mature discipleship is not when we move on from the gospel to understand deeper things; it's when we understand the gospel more deeply. It's been said that a person who understands the gospel clearly will experience it as "My chains fell off," not "I better not mess this up."[8] Just as Paul had to fill in the gaps of gospel understanding in Corinth and Galatia, so it is the job of the leader to help others live their whole lives in response to the whole gospel of Jesus Christ.

Responding to a Girl Named Grace

When Grace pulled up to Mike and me on that fateful rainy night in Yellowstone, she asked, "If I let you in, you are not going to kill me, are you?" My guess is that if we had answered yes, she would have sped away. And she would have been completely justified in her decision. She would have made it to Grant Village safely, but we would have been left as we were.

The gospel is the announcement that Jesus Christ has come. He knows the answer to the question: "If I let you in, you are not going to kill me, are you?" He already knows that we will. He would have been justified if he had sped away from us. And yet, because of his love, he doesn't. The gospel declares that Christ opens the door, invites us to climb in just as we are so that he can get us safely to the place we long to be. Along the way, as we more deeply understand what God has done for us, we begin to be transformed—created anew to what God has in mind for us to each become.

One last footnote to the night Grace rescued Mike and me. Later that night we ran into her again in the cafeteria at the inn. We found ourselves returning to one phrase over and over again: "Thank you. Thank you for what you have done for us."

If you have never made a decision to respond to the good news of who God is and what he has done, what is holding you back? Maybe this could be a holy moment for you, the moment when your eyes are opened to grace and spark a life of gratitude as you follow Christ. God loves you enough to send his one and only Son, Jesus Christ, so that you might not perish but have everlasting life. It's pretty mind-blowing news, isn't it? I once did not believe, but I was curious enough to ask the right questions, and God used those questions to lead me to himself in Christ. Jesus said he has come so that we might have life and have it to the fullest. I do not want you to miss out on that, and it can begin now.

Here's a simple prayer you can pray (or use your own words) to express to God your desire to trust in what Jesus has done. After you pray, I encourage you to find a local church that teaches the Bible and trusts that Jesus is the way back to God. Get involved with them, and tell them about your new decision.

Lord,

Thank you that you see me—all of me: the good, the bad, and the ugly parts of me. Thank you that you do not just see me, but that you love me. Thank you for sending your Son, Jesus Christ, to be the way that I could be made right with you. Please forgive me of my sin because of what Jesus accomplished on the cross. Give me the new nature that you promise for those who are created anew. Fill me with your Holy Spirit to empower me to follow you all the days of my life.

In Jesus' name,
Amen

Questions Worth Being Curious About

1. Dallas Willard asks those who do not accept Christ as Lord, "Would you *like* it if Jesus turned out to be Lord?" What is your answer to that question? Why or why not?

2. If you are a follower of Jesus, think of one person you know who does not accept Christ as Lord. Are you willing to ask them Willard's question? Why or why not? How does the prospect of asking them that question make you feel? Scared, excited, worried, or something else? Why is that?

3. Which half of the gospel are you more likely to accept? God loves you as you are (embrace)? Or God loves you too much to leave you that way (transformation)? Why is that? How does that affect your life of discipleship?

4. The gospel is not just the thing that saves us; it's also the thing that matures us. Have you experienced that to be true in your life? Why or why not? What might God be inviting you to do with that realization?

5

THE IDENTITY QUESTION: WHO AM I, ANYWAY?

If you want a wise answer, ask a reasonable question.
JOHANN WOLFGANG VON GOETHE

"Well then, who are you?" they asked.
JOHN 1:21

My oldest sister was eighteen when I was seven. One night she was babysitting me in my parents' home, and it was time for bed, so she told me to head upstairs to my bedroom. She would be up in a few moments, she assured me, to tuck me in.

Heading upstairs from the first to the second floor of our home was always a bit daunting to me at age seven. I would stand at the bottom of that dark staircase, my heart beating a bit faster, wondering what boogeyman was awaiting me upstairs.

Thankfully, there was a light switch at the bottom of the staircase that turned on the light at the top. So I flipped the light on and headed up the steps. My habit was to stand in the lit hallway and then reach my hand around the door frame to grope for the light switch in my bedroom; that way I did not have to go into the room in the dark. I had an active imagination, and always at that moment I worried that whatever monster was lurking in my bedroom would reach out and grab me. I told my little seven-year-old mind to not be afraid, however, because I had done this hundreds of times, on hundreds of other nights, and nothing had happened.

Until this night.

I reached my little hand around the door frame and flipped the switch. Just as I did, I saw three strangers wearing pantyhose over their heads. One of them quickly grabbed me, covered my mouth, and held me down, telling me to be quiet. Needless to say, I was terrified. I started to kick and squirm and bite the hand covering my mouth.

As I was fighting with all my might, the three strangers took off the pantyhose covering their heads. They were, it turned out, three of my sister's friends; they had broken into our home through an unlocked second-story window as a joke to scare my sister.

Once I saw who they were, I immediately knew I had nothing to be afraid of: These were friends. I went from the sheer terror of fighting abductors to the sheer excitement of being in on the joke.

Sometimes, knowing someone's identity can make all the difference.

Answering the Identity Question

A clear sense of identity is one of the most important things a leader needs in order to lead others well. How we answer the question of who we are will affect not just our own sense of identity, but also things such as our character, our decision-making, and ultimately how we interact with others. The trinity of identity, character, and decision-making affects everything we do, everything we say, and all that we will create through our efforts. Jesus points out, "A good tree produces good fruit, and a bad tree produces bad fruit" (Matthew 7:17). Who we are on the inside will eventually show up on the outside. Author Wayne Cordeiro once said it this way: "You teach what you know, but you reproduce who you are."[1]

The simplest way to begin to discover who you are is to know who you *are not*. We all remember taking multiple-choice tests as kids. They were my favorite because you knew the answer was in there somewhere—you just had to find it. Even if you were not certain of the answer immediately, you could at least make some progress by narrowing out all the incorrect answers.

The same is true with discovering who you are. Crossing off the options of who you know you are not is progress in discovering who God created you to be.

Knowing who you *are not* gives you the permission to say no to others (and yourself), which is a critical skill. Knowing who you *are not* allows you to focus on who you are and what God created you to be and do. This may actually be divinely hardwired into us. As infants grow, they begin to enter a stage called *separation and individuation*.[2] An infant has experiences that help him separate himself from others— to distinguish between "me" and "not-me." Psychologists tell us that when it comes to identity formation in infants, "you can't have a 'me' until you first have a 'not-me.'"[3]

John the Baptist was a phenomenal leader. People were coming in droves to hear him and doing what he taught them. That is pretty impressive for a guy who ate bugs. He was creating such a stir that the Jewish leaders sent priests and temple assistants from Jerusalem to ask him, "Who are you?"

He came right out and said, "I am not the Messiah."

"Well then, who are you?" they asked. "Are you Elijah?"

"No," he replied.

"Are you the Prophet we are expecting?"

"No."

JOHN 1:19-21

The second part of the identity-forming process we all experienced as infants is called *individuation*. This has to do with establishing not only who we are *not* but also who we *are*. The Scriptures pointed this out long before psychologists discovered it. John, for example, was clear about who he was not, but also about who he was. He was asked, "Then who are you? . . . What do you have to say about yourself?"

John replied in the words of the prophet Isaiah:

"I am a voice shouting in the wilderness,
  'Clear the way for the LORD's coming!'"

JOHN 1:22-23

John knew who he wasn't, and that was part of the key to discovering who he was. John was the voice shouting in the wilderness. Jesus was the one he was clearing the way for.

Two Questionable Ways to Answer the Identity Question

When it comes to answering the question of who we are, all of us have some source that we commit to as our authority. As John Ortberg noted, "There is no such thing as an uncommitted person."[4] All of our answers to any of our questions are founded on something or someone. The two most common ways that people tend to answer the identity question is by what other people say, and what we have done. Both of these sources are worth careful scrutiny, not because they are always wrong, but because they are not always right.

The moment you begin to relate to others, they will begin to form opinions about who you are. This is natural, normal, and even good. But if the identity question is left blank in your heart, those opinions easily become the *basis* for your identity. These opinions may come with good or bad intentions; most of these opinions are formed without conscious thought; those who are shaping your identity often do so without knowing they are doing anything at all. You will be pressed to become who others want you to be to help them out, to meet a need, to live up to an expectation they have, or simply to keep your job. It's a recipe for chaos and confusion, depending on who is in the room and whether they hold a high or low opinion of you.

John the Baptist was present when Jesus experienced the Holy Spirit descending on him at his baptism. John affirmed that Jesus was the Chosen One of God (John 1:32-34). Similarly, when Jesus asked his disciples, "Who do you say I am?" Peter correctly identified him as the Messiah (Luke 9:20). John and Peter were correct in their opinion about Jesus' identity, but that's not the challenge. The challenge is that others will get our identity wrong. Some thought Jesus was John the Baptist come back to life; others thought he was Elijah or one of the other ancient prophets; still others thought Jesus was in league with the Devil (Luke 9:19; 11:15). What if Jesus had based his identity on what *those* people thought of him? Clearly, we need to get the question of our identity answered by something more stable than people's opinions if we are going to lead well for the long run.

The second source that we tend to turn to in answering the question of who we are is what we have done. Accomplishments are a good thing. Adam and Eve were given work to do in the Garden of Eden before they fell into sin. God has prepared good things in advance for us to do (see Ephesians 2:8-10). However, using our track record of accomplishments as the primary source of our identity is worth questioning because eventually even the most remarkable leaders fail. Just because you failed once does not make you a failure forever.

Even in our successes, however, Jesus points us beyond our track record to something more stable on which to base our identity. When a group of seventy-two people from Jesus' leadership core returned from a successful short-term mission trip, they joyfully declared, "Lord, even the demons obey us when we use your name!" Jesus' answer to them clues us in on a better way to answer our identity question than simply what other people think or what we have accomplished. After affirming that they had in fact made a significant difference for the Kingdom of God, he redirects them: "But don't rejoice because evil spirits obey you; rejoice because your names are registered in heaven" (Luke 10:17-20). In other words, there is something greater than accomplishments (even those done in Jesus' name) when it comes to answering the identity question.

The Truest Thing About You

If the opinions of others and the accomplishments of our efforts are not consistent enough to tell us who we are, then what can bear the weight of that question? Both John the Baptist and Jesus answered the question of who they were by listening to God's word to them. In the case of John, he heard God's word through the prophet Isaiah. In Jesus' case, we are told that after his baptism, "as Jesus came up out of the water, the heavens were opened and he saw the Spirit of God descending like a dove and settling on him. And a voice from heaven said, 'This is my dearly loved Son, who brings me great joy'" (Matthew 3:16-17). When it comes to our identity, *the truest thing about us is what God says about us.*

Now, for many of us this does not happen by literally hearing a voice from heaven as the Spirit of God descends on us like a dove. Instead it happens through learning what the Scriptures teach us about our identity. For example, in Christ, we can become children of God who can pray and say "Our Father" (John 1:12-13; 1 John 5:1; see also Matthew 6:9). We become not just children of God, but also children of God whom he clearly loves and for whom he affirms his love throughout his Word (see Galatians 1:4; 1 John 3:1). As Tim Keller puts it, "You're not just becoming a nicer person or a more disciplined person or a more moral person. . . . You're becoming a more complete person, the person you were designed to be. The person you were ransomed to be."[5]

Jesus is about to launch the greatest leadership endeavor in global history, but instead of speaking to him about leadership tips, God the Father speaks to him about who he is. God affirms three things about Jesus' identity:

1. He is God's Son.
2. He is dearly loved.
3. He brings God the Father great joy.

The point is not that Jesus didn't know who he was before God spoke these things to him. When he was twelve, Jesus already understood that he was God's Son (see Luke 2:49). The point is that knowing who you are is foundational—for your own life, and also for those you lead.

The truest thing about you is that you are a beloved child of God.

Let that sink in for a moment. That's your identity if you are in Christ.

It's easy to dismiss this as something that God the Father feels only toward Jesus, and not a person like you or me. Certainly, God the Father and Jesus had a unique relationship. Christ is divine, and we are not. Jesus never sinned, and we all have sinned. However, God's love for us is firm, certain, and the foundation of our identity. As Jesus himself taught us, God so loved the world that he gave his one and only Son, so that everyone who believes in him will not perish but have eternal life (John 3:16). The prophet Zephaniah speaks of God taking delight in his people, with his love calming our fears, and rejoicing over us with joyful songs (Zephaniah 3:17).

God loves you enough to sing.

The Discipleship Trinity: Identity, Character, and Decision-Making

At his baptism, Jesus had heard God the Father's word to him about his identity: He was God's Son, he was beloved, and he brought the Father great joy. Case closed, right? Not so fast.

Immediately following God the Father's affirmation of Jesus' identity, the Holy Spirit leads Jesus into the wilderness, where he fasts for forty days and nights, and then is tempted by the Devil. It's a pattern in the Scriptures for us to note: First comes the word, then comes the test.[6] This is where identity intertwines with the twin discipleship engines of character and decision-making.

The word *character* comes to us from Greek culture. A character was a stamping tool used by an artisan to give his creation a distinguishing mark. Similarly, God has stamped something into us, seeking for our identity to grow into our character and ultimately our decision-making. The enemy comes to test just whether we will live by that distinguishing mark.

Satan's first two lines of temptation are intended to cause Jesus to base his identity on something other than what God the Father has said. Satan begins, "If you are the Son of God, tell these stones to become loaves of bread" (Matthew 4:3). In other words, be powerful. Then after taking Jesus to the highest point of the temple, Satan suggests that Jesus' identity will be proven when angels support his audacious acts: "If you are the Son of God, jump off!" (verse 6). In other words, be spectacular. Finally, the devil offers Jesus all the kingdoms of the world and their glory if Jesus will kneel down and worship him (see verse 9). In other words, be popular.

The moment we answer the identity question with the truth that we are God's beloved, our character and decision-making will be tested to see whether we base our sense of identity on what God has said or on alternate things such as success, power, or popularity. This is especially true for leaders. Henri Nouwen's insights on the topic are helpful:

> Success, popularity, and power can indeed present a great temptation, but their seductive quality often comes from the way they are part of a much larger temptation of self-rejection. We have come to believe in the voices that call us worthless and unlovable, then success, popularity, and power are easily perceived as attractive solutions. Self-rejection is the greatest enemy of the spiritual life because it contradicts the sacred voice that calls us the "Beloved." Being the Beloved constitutes the core truth of our existence.[7]

As God helps us to fully integrate our identity as the beloved of God within our actions, our character and decision-making are transformed. As Les Csorba rightly noted, "Leadership is character in motion."[8] Warren Buffet offers this insight:

> Somebody once said that in looking for people to hire, you look for three qualities: integrity, intelligence, and energy. And if they don't have the first, the other two will kill you. You think about it; it's true. If you hire somebody without [integrity], you really want them to be dumb and lazy.[9]

In other words, no matter how gifted we are, without character, everything eventually falls apart.

Living and Leading from Love

As we more deeply embrace God's declaration that we are his beloved in Christ, and allow him to stamp us with that distinctive mark, how we handle decisions will change. A person who starts off with her identity secure because of what God has said is a very different person from one who is still trying to secure her identity. It's one thing to lead because you are beloved and seek to share the good news with others; it's something very different to lead hoping that you will *become* beloved. People who lead from what God has said have a different quality of authority about them.[10] What does this look like? Let me mention three ways that living and leading from knowing God loves you makes a difference in everyday reality.

First, living and leading from love will free you to focus on what you want *for* people rather than *from* them. A person who does not settle the identity question based on what God has declared will become driven to validate her worth through acts of success, power, or popularity. When that happens with leaders, the leader will be out to prove something, not to serve someone. Christ taught that to be the greatest, we must become a servant of all (see Matthew 20:25-27; 23:11). When a person knows he is beloved of God, then he is free to lead others because of what he wants *for* them, not what he wants *from* them. Jesus himself said that he came not to be served, but to serve. To genuinely desire to serve others comes from the security of knowing that you are already loved; your identity is already established.

Second, living and leading from love will make you *more stable in your own discipleship and your leadership of others*. It's been said everyone loves you until you lead. The reality is that leadership requires making decisions, which some people will like and others will not. If your leadership and decision-making is up for grabs with the changing opinions of the crowd, then you will have erratic leadership. The only thing worse for people than no leadership is insecure, erratic leadership.

Jesus was not thrown by the normal ups and downs of people's opinions about who he was. He already knew what God the Father had said on that topic. His worth and identity were not up for a vote. His character and integrity were trustworthy. He was not more the beloved Son of God when throngs listened to him teach nor less the beloved Son of God when followers walked away. There are times when a course correction is needed, but if we are preoccupied by the hope that we will be able to make all people happy all the time, our leadership will suffer. Even Jesus could not make everybody happy all the time.

Having the identity question answered by God rather than other people allowed Jesus the stability to assess others' opinions in light of the deeper, more stable truth of God's Word. When Peter declared that Jesus was the Messiah, Jesus told him that he's blessed because he learned that from God the Father (Matthew 16:17). Jesus was able to assess Peter's response as being from God the Father because it matched what God had affirmed about Jesus before he launched his leadership efforts.

Interestingly, of the four questions Jesus answered directly (rather than cryptically, or by responding with a question of his own), one dealt specifically with his identity. Prior to his crucifixion, he was asked by the high priest, "Are you the Messiah, the Son of the Blessed One?"

"I Am," said Jesus. (You can't get a more direct answer than that.) And then he went on. "And you will see the Son of Man seated in the place of power at God's right hand and coming on the clouds of heaven" (Mark 14:61-62).

Answering the question of identity is not only a primary internal task in our souls; it is also a repeating task. God affirms Jesus' identity prior to Jesus' public ministry launch. But God later affirms Jesus' identity again, saying, "This is my dearly loved Son, who brings me great joy" (Matthew 17:5). God says this prior to Jesus' darkest hour—when he is betrayed by a close friend, his other disciples scatter, and he is hung on the cross. It's often before our greatest challenges that we need the deepest affirmation of God's love for us. Again, we see that first comes the word, and then comes the test. Last time God's affirmation provided endurance in the wilderness; this time it provided strength to face the cross.

Third, living and leading from love will empower you with *greater joy in life and leadership*. With the fact that life includes overcoming so many difficulties, challenges, and even persecutions, it can be easy to lose a sense of joy. At one point, Jesus is speaking to those who are and will be leaders in his Kingdom. He tells them that he loves them, tells them to remain in his love, and then says, "I have told you these things so that you will be filled with my joy. Yes, your joy will overflow!" (John 15:9-11). It's knowing and being reminded that you are the beloved of God that gives the power to experience joy even in the challenges of life, and also in those challenges to our leadership, as God allows us to influence others.

The Difference Maker

Remember when my sister's friends grabbed me that fateful night when I was seven? I was frantic and scared because I did not know who they were. I did not know how to respond. To know how to lead, you have to know who *you* actually are. When it comes to leadership, knowing your identity as the beloved of God makes all the difference. With God's help, it will make a difference in your character and then your decision-making. It will not only make a difference in your life, but also in the lives of those that God has placed around you. As Frank Laubach once observed, "The simple program of Christ for winning the whole world is to make each person he touches magnetic enough with love to draw others."[11] Knowing you are the beloved, and living with increasing constancy from that truth, will make you a person worth following.

Questions Worth Being Curious About

1. What would you say is the truest thing about you? Why would you say that? Where does that statement come from? How does it compare with what God's Word says about you?

2. Is there anywhere in your life you do not feel like you "measure up"? How does that make you feel? What do you do with those feelings when they come? How can those feelings lead you back to the good news of what God has done for us?

3. What are you tempted to base your identity upon apart from what God has said and done? Why is that? How do you live, feel, and act differently when you base your identity on something other than what God has said and done?

6

THE DISCERNMENT QUESTION: HOW WILL I MAKE DECISIONS?

We thought we had the answers, it was the questions we had wrong.

BONO

---

*My greatest strength as a consultant is to be
ignorant and ask a few questions.*

PETER DRUCKER

HAVE YOU EVER MADE A REALLY BAD DECISION? Let me take it one step further. Have you ever made a really bad decision that at the time seemed like a good one? Of course you have. Who hasn't?

One year I was in Pittsburgh in December on break from my college studies. I reconnected with one of my old friends, and we planned a several-night backpacking trip on the Laurel Highlands Hiking Trail, in the higher elevations of the mountains east of Pittsburgh. The trail has three-sided, wooden shelters, so we knew we would not have to sleep out in the open on the cold ground. It was cold with a light dusting of snow in Pittsburgh, but we were hardy souls. A little cold never hurt anyone, right?

We set up a plan to get dropped off at a starting point and then picked up three days later at a different point along the trail. There was quite a bit more snow in these higher elevations, it turned out, but with our backpacks, high-tech sleeping bags, and outdoors know-how, we remained confident and started off on the trail.

The trail was covered in a base of about three to four feet of old snow, but it was hard packed, so we were simply able to walk on top of it with no problems. About a mile in, however, the trail was noticeably less hard packed. Apparently all the day hikers who had traveled the trail before us had turned around at about that point. We were not day hikers, and we had no car to go back to, so we trudged ahead.

What we soon discovered was that we would take four or five steps on top of the snow pack, and then with our next step our foot would break through and sink down three or four feet. We'd pull our leg back out and start walking and it would happen again. And again. And again. Sometimes we were up to our hips in snowdrifts.

Our little jaunt of a winter backpacking trip turned into our own personal extreme backcountry adventure. Finally we arrived at the wooden platform lean-to that would be our shelter for the evening—much later than we had intended, thanks to our slow progress. We immediately started a fire to warm the shelter, ate some soup, and crawled into our sleeping bags for the night. My boots were sopping wet— so wet that when I took them off, water poured out of them.

I placed my boots close to the fire to dry them out for the next day.

At the time, it seemed like a good idea.

At about 4 a.m. I awoke to the smell of rubber burning. Our fire had shifted during the night and lit both of my boots on fire. The entire leather upper portion of the boots had burned completely; they did not exist anymore. The only thing that was left was the smoldering, melting, black-smoke-producing rubber outsoles.

How was I going to continue our seven-mile hike through the snow to the next shelter? We looked at the map and realized we were about one and a half miles to the nearest local road. So I had the joy of hiking through snow with improvised "boots" made up of trash bags, socks, and the leftover rubber flaps from the fire, tied together with a clothesline. We made it to the road and called our ride to come pick us up early.

Just because a decision seems like a good one at the time does not mean it will be. So the question then becomes not just what decision should I make at any given moment, but how can I make the wisest decisions most often?

The Decision Before the Decisions

There are people who have made the decision to study decisions. They tell us that on average, excluding habitual actions like brushing our teeth or eating breakfast, we make seventy conscious decisions a day.[1] That's 25,550 willful, conscious decisions a year. Over seventy-five years, that is 1,916,250 decisions. Anything you'll do almost two million times, it's worth asking how you'll do it.

Just because a decision seems good does not always mean it is good. In fact, according to one study, half of the decisions people make fail.[2] In other words, on average, there are a million opportunities for improvement.

Proverbs tells us there is a path before each person that seems right, but it ends in death (Proverbs 14:12; 16:25). All of our lives are packed with decisions to be made that create and affect everything we do. It's not enough to just hope that you will make good decisions. There is too much at stake. We need to be curious about how good decisions are made, both because our curiosity will lead to us making better decisions moving forward, and because it will help us teach others whom we serve how they can make better decisions.

The questions we ask about our decision-making process will be the single largest factor in how we answer all the other questions we face. In other words, it's the decision that will inform all the other decisions. It is an exponential decision. With that in mind, how can we make good, or even great, decisions as they come our way?

Prayer: Never Make a Decision Without God

The Scriptures are clear that God desires to guide us in our decisions. We are told, "If you need wisdom, ask our generous God, and he will give it to you. He will not rebuke you for asking" (James 1:5). God is interested in giving us the wisdom we need. This might seem so rudimentary that it's not worth mentioning, and yet, the reality is that many times good and even great people can allow the pressures of life to provoke them to skip this step. It's one thing to know something, quite another to actually do it.

God had commanded the Israelites to not make alliances with the surrounding nations as they entered into the land God promised to give them. The people of Gibeon, however, feared being destroyed, so they set out to trick the Israelites into an alliance. Though they lived nearby, they dressed in ragged clothes and worn-out sandals; they carried dry and moldy bread in worn-out saddlebags. Joshua, who was leading the Israelites, examined the food and other provisions, and noting they were old and weathered, decided it would be good to make a treaty with them. But Joshua had been commanded to not enter into such treaties. Joshua was a great leader, trusted by Moses, and selected by God to be Moses' successor. He had a history of making many good and even great decisions. But in this case, he and the Israelites made a bad call because they "did not consult the LORD" (Joshua 9:14). Anyone, even a great leader, can slide into what seems to be a good decision, only later to regret it.

The wisest decision begins with talking to God. This includes not only praying, but also considering what God teaches in the Scriptures and applying those teachings to your particular situation. Prayer includes humility, the willingness to ask questions without assuming we already know the answers, and the ability to listen.

When it comes to making good decisions, we must cultivate a trusting attitude toward God. Prayer helps us do this. He is the one who has the power to give wisdom. Our part is not simply to know that, but to practice it, by asking God to give us wisdom with the decisions we face. Often we can slide into thinking that we can guess what God would want us to do. Joshua thought so, but he thought wrong. Just because something seems like a good idea does not always mean it is.

Patience: Never Make a Rushed Decision

Good judgment not only comes through prayer; it comes by recognizing the importance of patience in discerning a wise decision. The number one cause of half of all organizational decisions that fail is making the decision prematurely.[3] Part of strong leadership is being calm when others are panicking, being patient under pressure. Patience in making a decision allows for information to be gathered, differing viewpoints to be weighed, and underlying issues to surface.

We can see this bit of wisdom from the biblical story of Daniel. Having been taken into captivity, Daniel was selected by his captors to be trained in their ways and culture. This included eating the food they were assigned, food that was forbidden to God's people. Daniel did not want to defile himself, but the chief of staff was concerned that the king would behead him if Daniel looked pale and thin compared to the others.

Daniel's input was, "Please test us for ten days on a diet of vegetables and water. . . . At the end of the ten days, see how we look compared to the other young men who are eating the king's food. Then make your decision in light of what you see" (Daniel 1:12-13). In other words, have some patience and allow things to be assessed. Sometimes the way to distinguish a good decision from a bad one is to test the decision, with a clear way out if the decision is not working out as hoped.

Obviously, there are times when deadlines loom and certain urgencies press for a decision to be made. A wise person's patience is proportional to the decision being made. The larger the decision, the more patiently it should be made. Small decisions can be made more quickly because a bad decision won't last as long or affect as much. Deciding where to go for dinner can be done quickly. Deciding whom to hire (or invite to be a volunteer leader) will take more time. The effects of a regretful dinner choice will only last for an evening, but the effects of a regretful addition to your leadership team will last longer.

Some decisions have quick deadlines, but not as many as we think. Often people will allow time even for a timely decision. But even if they do not, the lifelong decision to not rush decisions will certainly outweigh the benefits of a few missed opportunities that demand an immediate long-term commitment. For example, let's say that you are interested in recruiting a particular person to a particular role. As best you can tell, it fits them, they will be interested, and they will do a good job. Even with all of that in place, humility on your part (as well as their part) is to recognize that neither of you will really know how it will work out until some time passes. Both of you will benefit by making a final decision after the benefit of a test run.

Oftentimes, when I am talking with someone whether about stepping into a volunteer role or a paid staff role, we agree to a set period of time, after which we decide whether it's a good fit. A volunteer knows that they do not have to be committed to the role forever. After a year we meet to discuss their experience and thoughts. They are free to step out if it was a bad fit or not what they expected it to be. Likewise, I get to see if my initial impression actually holds true in reality.

As the Scriptures teach us, patience is better than pride (Ecclesiastes 7:8). Proportional patience means that the more far-reaching the decision, the more freedom you need to feel not to rush it.

People: Never Make a Decision Alone

In addition to giving counsel directly from his Word and through prayer, God will often use the right questions asked of the right people to guide us toward good decisions. Proverbs tells us that "plans succeed through good counsel;

don't go to war without wise advice" (20:18). The ability to ask questions and then listen well is key to making better decisions. There is a difference, however, between counsel and *wise* counsel. It's not enough to get advice; the advice has to be *good*.

So, how do we do that? How do we know who are the "right people" to ask for counsel? I think Jesus tips us off: "Wisdom is shown to be right by its results" (Matthew 11:19). In other words, look for people who are living the kind of life that indicates that they have been asking the right questions.

A number of years ago, a twentysomething in our church did something I consider remarkable because it is so rare. After a string of broken dating relationships, she came to the realization that "my boyfriend picker is broken." I was curious how she came to that conclusion. So I asked her some questions: How did she think good marriages happen? Why do some marriages seem to struggle less than others? Led by questions like these, she considered her past patterns and identified three married couples that she had been around enough to know that they had the kinds of marriages she hoped to have one day herself. She took the initiative and asked each of the three couples to give her feedback on her dating life—including what she called "veto power" over any guys that might just be the symptom of her "broken boy-friend picker."

One of the couples mentioned a guy she knew but previously assumed would not be the right fit. This led to more questions: Why do you think that? What assumptions are you making about who he is? What assumptions are you making about who would be compatible with you? How do you respond to the fact that the people you thought would be a right fit have not turned out to be that for you? Is what you are valuing in a guy right now going to be an obstacle to what you will value in five years or ten or twenty as your life stages change? In other words, how will you select based not just on what matters in this moment, but what will matter for a lifetime of companionship and marriage?

The decision of whether to pursue this guy was hers to make, but she did not make the decision alone. She knew what God's Word taught, had prayed for wisdom in this area of her life, and had invited some others into her discernment process. That was an act of humility. She freely was admitting that she did not know it all.

The couples she spoke with did not pretend to have all the answers either. Instead, their humility was shown in simply being willing to ask the right kinds of questions that God then used to help move her along in her process of discernment. Sometimes inviting the right people to give you counsel and ask the right questions can start you down the road to a decision that you might have not made left on your own. In that case, she and the guy started to date, and today (after taking time to get to know each other well) they are married.

The right person for input on one decision might not be the right person for input in a different area. For example, my wife and I have several couples that we admire for the qualities they have instilled in their high school kids. Having three young children, we are already asking for their input on raising our children and preparing ourselves for the high school years. The people we ask about parenting, however, are not the same people we rely on for wise counsel on leadership questions or financial issues. You want a great mechanic working on your car, and a great dentist working on your teeth. It's not very wise to invite a great mechanic to work on your teeth.

You do not have to *know* the right person personally to consider their perspective on a decision you may be facing. Sometimes the right person might have lived hundreds of years before you. I have "go to" theologians that I have never met, but I rely on them for theological questions. For example, one of the very best people in terms of considering the process of discernment is Ignatius of Loyola. His insights into when you can trust your feelings and when you need to not trust your feelings in the midst of discernment are brilliant.[4] I have never met him, but his spiritual exercises have deeply influenced how I understand discernment. It's just one of the reasons why books are so beautiful: We have access to the wisdom of people we may never have the privilege of personally knowing.

One specific way that I try to never make a decision alone is by meeting with a spiritual director trained in the Ignatian exercises. He is trained to ask me questions that will help me pay attention to my own soul as well as what God is inviting me into within my life. Our meetings are mainly him asking me questions: what I felt in a certain situation, why I felt it, and where I see God in the midst of it. His questions help me explore my own feelings, what the causes of them are, and specifically whether I feel the specific feeling when I have God at the conscious center of my life or when I have pushed him to the margin of my life. It's a very organic process of give and take, which often results in realizations that I would not have reached with my own self-generated questions.

Process: Never Waste a Bad Decision

In addition to prayer, patience, and people, good decisions are often the end result of a good process. When the Scriptures speak of good judgment, they often speak of it as a process. Psalm 111:10 tells us, "Fear of the LORD is the foundation of true wisdom. All who obey his commandments will *grow* in wisdom" (emphasis added). Proverbs tells us, "Whatever else you do, *develop* good judgment" (4:7, emphasis added). In other words, there is a process involved in becoming a better decision-maker. The passing of time alone is not enough. Everyone gets older, but have you noticed that not everyone gets wiser? Have you ever been curious about why that is the case?

One of the best ways to grow in wisdom and develop good judgment is to never waste a bad decision. Wasting a bad decision happens when we end our reflection with "I should have made a different decision." Processing a bad decision with the right questions can lead to better decision-making in the future. Curiosity about how God can redeem a bad decision similarly can be the foundation of a better decision-making process. If that happens, it will be the best bad decision you ever made.

Some examples of good questions about bad decisions follow:

- "How did I get to the point where I thought that was a good decision?"
- "What did I not see? What did I misunderstand? What was I missing?"
- "What changes to my decision-making process would have led to a better decision?"
- "Did I allow fear, anger, envy, or other emotions to set me up for a bad decision? If so, what can I do to be more aware of my underlying emotions and their effects on my decision-making the next time around?"
- "Is there anything I learned from this bad decision that can help me in other decisions I am facing or may face in the future?"
- "Whom did I process the decision with prior to acting? Did I have the right people around the table? Did they ask me the right kinds of questions to help me consider things from alternative angles?"

Of course, we can ask similar questions of a good decision. But most of us tend to feel greater urgency to examine our decisions that have not turned out as we had hoped. As a pastor, I have had many people come to me to process a problem or decision that did not work out well. I cannot remember a single time I have had a person come wanting to process a great success or a wise proactive decision. I wonder why that is.

Remember my attempt to try to dry my boots a little too close to the fire? It clearly was not the wisest decision. I could have simply decided: "Note to self: Do not do that again." I have in fact decided that, and it's resulted in some remedial growth of wisdom in my life. However, using questions to process that decision more deeply allowed me to see ways that the lessons of that cold night can apply to other, more important decisions. For example, what role did exhaustion play in that decision? Are there any other areas of my life where I am allowing weariness to affect my judgment? Why is it that I, like so many I know in our culture, jam-pack my schedule, leaving little margin and leading to great weariness—even when I know weariness not only isn't fun, but can set the stage for poor decisions? How can I set up a process where I make most of my decisions when I am the least tired?

I am by no means perfect at guarding myself and those I lead from decisions made out of weariness, but I'm much better now than I was then. I know it's just a simple story, but processing that one unwise decision well with the right questions has led to better decisions in a wide range of other areas.

The Stakes of Decision-Making

The longer you live, the more decisions you will make. If your leadership flourishes, then each decision you make will affect more and more people. With that in mind, it's critical to determine how you will make decisions. Not all ideas that seem good at the time end up actually being good decisions. It's critical for us to ask ourselves in advance how we can make good decisions when the time comes. What you learn from asking the right questions may be different from what I've learned, but I hope you will include prayer, patience, the right people, and the right process as a foundation. Then you will no longer be shackled to impulsive hunches, what just seems like a good idea at the time. The stakes of your life and those you influence around you are too high to make decisions without first asking how good decisions are made.

Questions Worth Being Curious About

1. How do you normally make decisions? Why do you make them that way? What assumptions exist underneath your way of making decisions?

2. What role does prayer play in your decision-making process? Do you find it hard or easy to take your decisions to God in prayer? What obstacles do you

face that hinder you from doing that? Is there anything you can do to reduce or remove those obstacles?

3. Have you ever rushed into a decision you regretted later? How can you cultivate greater patience in your decision-making process? Does that feel like relief to you or a hardship? Why is that?

4. Do you tend to make decisions alone or with input from others? Why do you think that is your pattern? Who might you be able to include in your decisions that would ask you helpful questions?

5. After you make a decision and see the results, do you ever stop to process the decision? If not, why not? If so, how do you do that? Do you tend to process only bad decisions or both good and bad decisions? Why is that?

7

THE RECOVERY QUESTION: CAN OUR BAGGAGE BE USED FOR SOMETHING BETTER?

Questions are never indiscreet. Answers sometimes are.

OSCAR WILDE

Do you want to get well?

JESUS, IN JOHN 5:6 (NIV)

AIRPORTS ARE FASCINATING PLACES TO ME. I love to people-watch, and living in Los Angeles, there may be no better place to watch an amazing variety of people than Los Angeles International Airport. Every time I am there, I am amazed at how different everyone is. On a recent trip, I arrived with some time to spare, so I sat at the departing gate sipping a coffee, watching people pass. Different ages, different ethnicities, some walking alone, others walking in groups, some single, some married, some with kids, some without, some in a hurry, and some walking slowly. Everyone was so different as they moved through the airport to their destination. And yet, I noticed, we all had one thing in common: We all were carrying some form of baggage.

The kinds of bags were almost as diverse as the people. Some carried backpacks, briefcases, purses, or satchels. Others had even larger bags that they wheeled behind them. Many people traveled with more than one bag.

A while back, I read a newspaper interview with a TSA agent. Asked what he had learned from screening airline passengers, he replied, "People look so different on the outside, but when you open up their baggage, everyone carries the same stuff: toothpaste, toothbrush, clothes, and deodorant. Maybe we are not as different as we look on the outside."

Everyone I have ever met, beginning with me, is carrying baggage through life. *Baggage* is my term for all the things that others have done or said (or left undone or unsaid) that have created pain, hardship, and suffering in our lives. In other words, baggage is what results when sinners live near each other and relate to one another. Left unaddressed, this baggage weighs us down as we travel through life.

On the rarest of occasions, I will meet someone who claims that they have no baggage. That's the worst kind to have! If you do not know what you are carrying with you, then you will not do anything about it—or better yet, with it. We do not have the luxury of relating to people who are blank slates. Every person you will ever meet or have the privilege to influence has some kind of baggage in his or her life. Because that is the case, if you want to serve them well, you need to become an adept baggage handler: first dealing with your own baggage, and then helping others deal with theirs.

When it comes to our pains, disappointments, and heart-aches, our questions can be particularly powerful: What baggage am I carrying? Why am I carrying it? How is God inviting me to handle this baggage? Can my baggage be redeemed? Used for something better?

Baggage is in every story; however, with God's redeeming help, baggage does not have to be the end of the story.

Picking Up Baggage

I knew Mauricio as an acquaintance, but then a mutual friend shared more of his story with me. I could not believe it. I thought it must be exaggerated, so I called Mauricio and he told me his story directly.[1]

Mauricio was born in a small mountainous village in Nica-ragua, the youngest of twenty-five children who had many dif-ferent mothers but the same alcoholic father. Mauricio's mom gave birth to him under a tree and then threw him in a pit toilet—a deep hole in the ground with an outhouse built around it. She hoped he would drown in the excrement, but Mauricio landed on a plank of wood that kept him from drowning.

The families we are born into have the ability to affect us deeply and profoundly, whether for good or evil—and often some mixture of the two. It's my reality, it's your reality, and it's the reality of every single person you will ever meet. We all pick up pain and baggage. Admittedly, Mauricio's story is extreme, and one danger surrounding baggage is to get into comparing the depths of our pits. But the question that will move us forward in life is not "Who has been in the worst pit or carries the most baggage?" The question that holds the power to move us forward is, "Is it possible that, with God's healing and redeeming help, my pit does not have to be the end of my story?"

Mauricio was left in a pit. Maybe that's where you feel you've been left. Maybe you feel that way because of what your mom or dad, or your siblings, or a coworker, or even a stranger, did or left undone. Your pit could be financial, relational, emotional, or something else. Sometimes we find ourselves in a pit because we put ourselves there through our unwise choices. Other times, a whirlwind of circumstances has left us stuck. Whatever the case, most of us will log time in the pit at some point in life.

The One Who Lifts Us Out of Our Pits

Newborn Mauricio is still in the pit in Nicaragua. Some young boys are playing nearby and hear him crying, down in the pit, hanging on the plank of wood. They get their mom, who calls to a man nearby, who is working with a rope. The man ties the rope to a post and lowers himself into the pit, rescuing baby Mauricio from the excrement. Mauricio is adopted by his dad's sister, who moves to Los Angeles and raises him as part of her family. They become involved in a church in downtown Los Angeles.

Whether you are in a pit because someone else threw you down there or because you jumped into it by some bad decisions of your own, there is good news. *The pit (your baggage) does not have to be the end of your story.* Why not? Because God sees you in your pit and has different plans for you. Psalm 40 tells us that God specializes in lifting people out of the pit, out of the muck and mire. He sets our feet on solid ground, steadying us as we walk along.

The first step in dealing with our baggage is to look for God's work in our lives, because God is in the business of lifting us out of our pits.

When Mauricio is a teenager, he is told the truth of his story—how the woman he has called *Mom* is really his aunt. He falls into an emotional and spiritual pit, filled with misery inside himself. All the questions you would expect began to rise within him. "My dad doesn't love or accept me. How can I believe God is my Father who loves me? My mom discarded me in a pit toilet. Do I have any value to anyone?" He cries out to God, "What now?"

Then one day, flipping through the Bible, his eyes fall on these words:

> Even if my father and mother abandon me,
>   the LORD will hold me close.
>
> PSALM 27:10

This discovery leads to six years of Mauricio processing the truth that though his parents did not accept him or love him, he does not have to be defined by them. Through what

Jesus Christ did hanging from two planks of wood, God has received him, accepted him, and loved him. Because he has been loved and forgiven by Christ, and with the help of a small group of men and a wise Christian counselor, he is eventually able to love and forgive his parents.

Handling Our Baggage with God's Help

While each chapter of this book focuses on a single question, the questions that we ask are not sealed off into separate silos. They often overlap and interplay with each other in the real stories of our lives. For Mauricio, the questions of his baggage led to questions of the gospel, questions of his own identity, and more.

As part of his journey to forgiveness, Mauricio returned to Nicaragua and, with the help of his aunt, found his birth mother. He explained who he was and told her that he had forgiven her because of what Jesus did for him, and he handed her a New Testament.

This is the part of the story where I wish I could tell you she came to Christ and all is well. But she didn't. In fact, Mauricio's mom denied the whole thing, despite many people in the village confirming the story. People pointed out that she had been nine months pregnant and that something must have happened to the baby. She offered no answer.

Forgiveness of past wounds is an essential part of our story. We must not rush through it or past it. It took Mauricio many years to genuinely forgive all that had happened to him in a fully integrated way. Forgiveness is essential to our story, but it's not the end of the story.

It turns out that both the tree Mauricio was born under in this small mountain village and the pit toilet he was left in are still there. He sat down by the tree and prayed. "Well, God, this has not turned out like I thought. My mom hasn't come to know you. She denies everything. Why am I even down here? I need you to speak to me." Sometimes the best thing we can do is ask God a genuine, open-ended question, trusting that He will lead us through it.

Mauricio tells me that he felt God whisper in his heart: "You've done what I've asked." So he pulled open a Bible, sat with his back propped against the tree where he was born, next to the pit toilet where he was abandoned. He ended up reading these words:

> On each side of the river stood the tree of life, bearing
> twelve crops of fruit, yielding its fruit every month. And
> the leaves of the tree are for the healing of the nation.
> REVELATION 22:2, NIV

Those words led Mauricio to ask new, forward-moving questions: "God, what are you inviting me to in the midst of all of this? How can all of this baggage be used for something better—something redeemed by your goodness?" Each of these questions helped him move forward to a new chapter not only in his life, but soon into the lives of many others.

God can take your misery and turn it into a ministry to help others. In fact, ministry begins when we touch someone's misery for good in Jesus' name. What makes a person a leader is when they do not just deal with their own baggage, but when they also desire to help others to do the same with God's help. When we do that, we lead people toward the grace and redemption of God. The most powerful thing that happens to us is not what others have done or left undone that harmed us. In Christ, the most powerful thing that can happen is what God does with what has been done to us. He's like some kind of divine alchemist, turning the lead of baggage into the gold of something better.

Mauricio is now in the midst of living into the answer God has shown him. He is in the process of purchasing the land in Nicaragua where his greatest pain began, so he can create a children's home where low-income women can come for job training and prenatal and maternal care. If they decide to raise their child, they will be better equipped to do so. If they decide not to raise their child, they will have the option to give the child to the care of this children's home, so that never again will a child in that village end up thrown into a pit.

Baggage for Better: The Ongoing Story God Writes

As Mauricio shared his story with me, I could not help but think of parallels with the story of Joseph (see Genesis 37–50). Joseph was thrown in a pit not by his mom, but by his brothers. They hated Joseph in part because their dad favored him.

Their simmering anger was compounded as Joseph shared some dreams of his brothers bowing down to him. Clearly, Joseph had never been to a family dynamics class where he learned what was wise to say to your older brothers.

One of Joseph's brothers, Judah, made the argument that they should sell Joseph rather than kill him, so the brothers pulled Joseph out of the pit and sold him to slave traders headed to Egypt. There he was sold to an Egyptian, whose wife later falsely accused him of rape, and he was thrown in jail. From a pit to a jail cell is probably not what Joseph had in mind for his life. It's clear that he picked up some heavy baggage along the way. I can't even imagine all the questions running through his mind and heart during his years in jail.

After a long time in prison, Joseph correctly interpreted Pharaoh's dreams (with God's help), and as a reward Pharaoh placed Joseph in charge of all of Egypt. Joseph had two sons in Egypt, the first named Manasseh, which sounds like and may be derived from the Hebrew word for *forget*. "God," Joseph said, "has made me forget all my troubles and everyone in my father's family." He named his second son Ephraim, which sounds like the Hebrew word for *fruitful*, saying, "God has made me fruitful in this land of my grief" (Genesis 41:51-52). Joseph repeats the pattern we saw with Mauricio: Questions of forgiveness often precede questions of how our baggage can be redeemed. What God does *in* us becomes the foundation of what God will do *through* us.

Famine comes to the entire area, and true to Joseph's original dream, his brothers come bowing before Joseph, seeking grain for their families. They don't realize that Joseph is their brother, but he does, and through a series of events, Joseph brings his entire family to Egypt so that he can provide for them in the famine. His brothers expected to pay for their sins, but instead they are ambushed by grace. Joseph summarizes the wounds of his past: "You intended to harm me, but God intended it all for good. He brought me to this position so I could save the lives of many people" (Genesis 50:20).

Turning baggage to something better is not just God's story for Mauricio. It's an ongoing story that God has been writing throughout human history for those who turn their pain into prayerful questions.

The way that God transforms our baggage to something better, the way we become fruitful in the land of our grief, begins with forgiving the troubles that others have caused us. Everyone you know is carrying some wounds, but not everyone you know will ask God the questions that help clarify how God will turn that baggage into something better. With God's help, we can each settle yesterday's wounds and help others do the same.

Hope Wanted: Best Served as Questions

The question Jesus most often asked people was, "What do you want me to do for you?" (see, for example, Matthew 20:32). I have found this question to be the very best way to serve those processing pain, suffering, or the baggage in their story.

Sometimes people do not know what they want. Other times they are very clear: They simply want someone to be with them, to listen to them, to share the pain with them. During these fragile seasons, my experience is that cliché answers, even if true, are best left unsaid. For example, "We know that in all things God works for the good of those who love him" (Romans 8:28, NIV) is a true statement, but it will often come across as crass and without compassion, a quick fix to a complex problem. The person in pain may have trouble accessing its hope.

If you simply stay with the question of "What would you like me to do for you?" the answer from the person you are serving will change over time, which becomes an opportunity to help the person move forward. Rather than beginning with a predetermined plan, simply asking the right question to those in the midst of coping with the baggage of life can be a step in a redemptive direction.

Great souls grow slowly. They also do not grow without facing some kind of pain or suffering. In those fragile seasons, people are particularly receptive to open-ended questions. Joseph's story took decades to unfold. Mauricio's process of forgiveness took a full six years. Wise people know that healing takes time, but time alone does not heal people. There are many people who have experienced pain decades ago but never processed it with the help of open-ended questions from a caring friend. Here again, questions are often the best way to serve and lead the other person. A hopeful question allows them to arrive at the answer in their own time. For example, "Do you think God could bring about any good from this painful situation? What might that look like to you? Would you like to talk about that now, or save it for another time?"

Processing our personal pain through asking hopeful questions can often lead us to lead others in ways we never would have envisioned. Having a heart filled with compassion is the key to this. The word *compassion* literally means to "suffer with." Our compassion for others often comes through our own experience of pain. For example, as I have processed my grief over the loss of my father to his third battle with cancer, one of the things that has emerged is a great compassion for people whose loved ones receive a diagnosis of cancer. Sometimes from the ashes of our pain rises the redemption of serving others traveling the same road behind us. We ask the hopeful question, "Do you think God could bring anything good from this painful situation?" Oftentimes we discover the answer one day at a time as we walk with others who have experienced similar pain.

Our church has seen the power of regularly telling "baggage used for better" stories. It's become part of our culture. The more we do this, the more people seem to begin to look for God's invitation to use their misery for ministry, their grief for a greater good. Telling stories such as Mauricio's holds the implicit hopeful question: "Well, his pain was not the end of the story. What would it look like if my pain was not the end of my story either? Would I want that? Why or why not? If I do want that, how can I begin to explore that in my own life?"

We Are All in Recovery

Everyone you know has some pain, wound, baggage, or pit in their story. It's part of living in a world marred by sin. Leaders need to set the pace with those they lead by constantly asking how God can heal us, and in time changing the question to how God is inviting us to use our most painful places for something better. Sometimes the best part of the healing of wounds is knowledge that they are not being wasted.

The ways our baggage can be used for better are almost as varied as we are as people. Part of our job is to help others discover what that looks like in their own lives by pointing out and celebrating when it happens in others' lives. For example, the addict who is gaining higher ground helps sponsor others who are beginning the recovery process. For others, having been a loner in high school becomes the launching pad to reach out to students on the fringe now. A couple I know almost ended their marriage because of an affair. Now, having been reconciled to one another and God, they seek out other struggling marriages to offer hope and help. People who were far from God and now have been reconciled feel compelled to help others who are far from God come to know him. A woman who was never adopted is now married, and she and her husband have adopted two children into their home. A man in our church grew up without a dad; today, he is mentoring a boy in our neighborhood who is growing up without a dad. In each of those cases, no one gave them a quick answer. It took time and lots of questions centered on forgiveness that then led to new sets of hopeful questions as their misery became their own personal ministry.

The bad news is that we all have baggage. We all fall or get thrown into pits. But there is good news that is greater than the worst bad news. Through asking first prayerful questions of forgiveness and then hopeful questions of redemption, we can see God transform our baggage to something better. And when that happens, as it did for the psalmist, this will be what people can see. This will be the song that we sing through our lives:

> I waited patiently for the LORD;
> > he turned to me and heard my cry.
> He lifted me out of the slimy pit,
> > out of the mud and mire;
> he set my feet on a rock
> > and gave me a firm place to stand.
> He put a new song in my mouth,
> > a hymn of praise to our God.
> Many will see and fear the LORD
> > and put their trust in him.

PSALM 40:1-3, NIV

Questions Worth Being Curious About

1. What baggage do you carry that you sense God is inviting you to forgive or begin the process of forgiveness? Do you think forgiveness is even possible?

Why or why not? What is the biggest obstacle to forgiving that you are facing?

2. Have you ever experienced God bringing something good out of what others intended for harm? Does that give you hope that he can do that again? Why or why not?

3. Joseph said God made him fruitful in the land of his grief. Would you want that for yourself? If so, do you feel ready to ask God to do that? If so, take a moment and prayerfully ask him to help you live into ways your baggage can be used for something better in Jesus' name.

8

THE COMMUNITY QUESTION: WHAT ARE THE MARKS OF GROUPS THAT HELP PEOPLE FLOURISH?

It is error only, and not truth, that shrinks from inquiry.

THOMAS PAINE

Who is my mother? Who are my brothers?

JESUS, IN MATTHEW 12:48

WHAT'S YOUR FAVORITE TOM HANKS MOVIE? *Forrest Gump*? *The Green Mile*? *Toy Story*? *Saving Private Ryan*? *Saving Mr. Banks*? There are a lot of good ones. One of the best is *Cast Away*.

In *Cast Away*, Tom Hanks plays a FedEx agent who is the lone survivor of a plane crash somewhere over the South Pacific Ocean. He ends up on a deserted island for four years and is saved—by a volleyball. He names the volleyball Wilson in honor of its maker, and for four years, he carries on a conversation with it. At one point, he even argues with it. Wilson keeps him sane, until one of the most catastrophic scenes in the movie, when he loses Wilson overboard from his makeshift raft. When that happens, he deteriorates to the edge of insanity.[1] Why does that happen?

We were created for community. If you have ever given a child a time-out, then you have used our innate sense of community to alter your child's heart or behavior. Why does it work? Because we were created for community. The worst offenders in a jail might be sent to solitary confinement. Why is that considered such punishment and even torture? Because we are hardwired to do life together, not alone or apart.

The Power of the Right Kind of Community

The power of the right kind of community is one of the most constant themes of the Bible. God declares that it is not good for Adam to be alone (Genesis 2:18). Eve is created, and the first command God gives to them is to be fruitful and multiply (Genesis 1:28). Ecclesiastes tells us that "two people are better off than one, for they can help each other succeed. . . . Three are even better" (Ecclesiastes 4:9,12). Proverbs 27:17 tells us that friends sharpen each other, or help one another flourish. One of the first things Jesus does when launching his ministry is start a small group. To accept Jesus' invitation to follow him meant that you would be following him with others, not simply as a lone individual. We are told that the early church met together regularly doing a certain kind of life together, not alone or apart (see Acts 2:42).

God has called us not only to be individuals who believe in him but a community that belongs to him. If God's agenda includes the creation of a redemptive community, then we are wise to move in that direction. It's been observed that to swim a fast 100 meters, it's better to swim with the tide than work on your stroke.[2]

We were created for community, but not just any kind of community. We were created for a certain kind of community that God is making within and through those who are found in Jesus Christ. One of the sets of questions that we must ask, then, is how we can create space for ourselves and others not only to belong, but also to flourish.

A while back, I invited part of our leadership team to take some time away and discuss a cluster of questions centered on the topic of community. We were curious about why some small groups seem to flourish and others seem to quickly fall apart. If community is a primal drive for us as humans, why do we seem to have such a hard time with it? Why is it that someone can be around for years and yet not feel a deep sense of personal belonging in the church we lead? Apart from our own felt needs for community, are there any characteristics of community that Jesus invites us into?

Our goal was simply to try to distill from our experiences and the teaching of the Bible some guideposts for people to understand when it came to finding belonging as part of our community. We talked, read, prayed, and wrestled (well, not literally). We not only wanted people to feel a sense of belonging in their life groups, we wanted those groups to create disciples. I want to walk you through what we arrived at as a way to help you think about your own answer to the community question.

DR GLOO

We came to believe that creating space for people to belong within a flourishing community would require six core marks. We outline those six things with the acronym DR GLOO. (It rhymes with boo. We thought of making it GO LORD, but felt that DR GLOO was, um, stickier.) Let me walk you through what we think it will take to honestly and biblically answer what it will take for us as leaders to create space for people to flourish together. Hopefully it will stir your own thoughts on how you will answer that question.

We determined that personal belonging in a Christ-centered community is:

- Difficult, not easy
- Relational, not programmatic
- Giving, not simply taking
- Leadership-driven, not need-centered
- Open, not closed
- Outward, not inward alone

Difficult, not easy. One of the challenges we recognized is that most of the teachings we had ever heard (or given) on the topic of community were mainly designed to inspire people to move from increasingly individualized lives to see the importance and benefits of being in a community. The problem with that was that we often "oversold and underdelivered" on that front. When we overinspire while underpreparing people, we are not serving them well. In the long run, inspiration is enough to get you going, but not keep you going. When you forewarn people that community will be difficult, not easy, they are more likely to stick with it when the first relational challenges arise.

Doing the Christ-centered life with others is difficult, not easy. Anything worth doing in life is difficult, and relationships are no exception. Jesus' first disciples included those who were rabidly anti-Roman and those who worked with the Romans as tax collectors. They probably rubbed each other the wrong way from time to time. All relationships take time, commitment, and initiative, but we cannot let that scare us into isolation. The only thing more costly than doing community is not doing community.

When the gospel began to be announced to Gentiles, the challenges grew even further. The apostle Paul uses the picture of a temple being "carefully" built together (Ephesians 2:21). He says "carefully" because he understands that sometimes, some of us are a pain to be around. More accurately, some of the time *all* of us are a pain to be around.

When temple masons of old would build a temple, they would take rough-cut stones and chisel each of the stones until they fit together well. Sometimes the stones would be rubbed against each other to rub off the rough edges so they could fit more seamlessly. In a similar way, being part of God's temple can be difficult: Sometimes God uses the people who annoy us the most to shape us the most to be like him.

Relational, not programmatic. Jesus' primary invitation to his first disciples was to "come and follow me." The moment you decided to do that, you became part of a relational community. Paul tells us that in Christ "you are members of God's family" (Ephesians 2:19). Jesus himself redefined the whole idea of family when he said, "Who is my mother? Who are my brothers?" Then he pointed to his disciples and said, "Look, these are my mother and brothers. Anyone who does the will of my Father in heaven is my brother and sister and mother!" (Matthew 12:48-50).

The larger a group grows, the harder a leader needs to work to establish a relational community. The result is often the establishment of programs designed to do what happened more organically in the smaller group. The challenge is that programs do not help people belong; people help people belong. A sense of belonging grows not just through attending a weekend worship service or a small group, but when we use those gatherings as a chance to build real relationships with real people, with real names and real stories. Those relationships might begin in a programmed setting, but they soon reach beyond them into daily life.

Jose moved to Los Angeles a little over a year ago and started to come to Christian Assembly. He is married to

Maria, and they have one young daughter. Maria is pregnant with their second, but the latest pregnancy has been a difficult road for them. Maria is thirty weeks pregnant and is presently in the hospital as they are trying to hold off contractions. Needless to say, they are feeling the stress of the situation.

With all that was happening, Jose had not been able to make it to a weekend worship service for a number of weeks. Last weekend, he came mistakenly thinking our 9 a.m. service started at 9:30 a.m. He was a bit confused, wondering why he did not hear anyone singing. Wandering around the lobby, he was approached by a twentysomething guy who introduced himself to Jose, welcomed him, and asked him a bit about his story.

Really desiring to spend some time singing in worship, Jose decided to stay for the first part of the 11:15 a.m. service. A few minutes before the service, he found a seat and then was approached by another man in his forties. This guy welcomed Jose as well, asking him if he was a regular part of Christian Assembly, which was followed by a conversation about what was unfolding in Jose and Maria's life.

A woman to Jose's left was sitting by herself. She looked a bit nervous and was perhaps struggling a bit herself. She said to Jose, "Wow! It's amazing that a guy who does not even know you expressed such interest in your story." That led to Jose offering a hand of welcome to this woman as well. He told me, "Given the struggle in my own life, had I not been so relationally welcomed, I probably never would have reached out relationally to a person I did not know."

All of that happened because of the "program" of the weekend worship service. But none of that would have happened without each person turning the program into a chance to begin or continue a relationship with another person.

Giving, not simply taking. Have you ever been to a potluck dinner? Done well, they can be the most amazing experiences. People pull out all the stops to bring their very best dish to share with others. They can be experiences of joy and laughter as people sample all the goodness that is being shared. But not all potlucks turn out like that.

When I was in my twenties, part of my job included leading a college group. I was new to the role and did not know many of the students, so I decided that it would be great for us to have a potluck meal together. I proposed the idea to the group, and everyone agreed and seemed excited.

The evening of the potluck dinner came. Let's just say it was less than inspiring. One guy brought an open bag of Doritos. Another guy brought two burritos from Taco Bell, but "got hungry on the way over, so I took a few bites of one of them already." Several people showed up empty-handed, I guess assuming that the others would bring enough to make their negligence go unnoticed. We had a good laugh as we each ate a few slightly stale Doritos and nibbled on half-eaten burritos. We never did another potluck after that!

Creating biblical community is a bit like a potluck. If

everyone gives, then everyone gets. However, if no one gives, then no one gets. Since most of us have been conditioned by the consumerism of the marketplace, we can bring that teaching to our expectations of community. Our natural response can be to come asking, "What will we get out of it?" But what if we changed the question to "What am I willing to give to it?" If we are going to create space for other people to flourish, we have to be givers, not only takers.

Jesus is the one who said, "It is more blessed to give than to receive" (Acts 20:35). He is the one who creates the opportunity to belong to the family of God by *giving* his life away. Paul later models the same thing as he pours out his life so that others can know the gospel and then belong to the community of God. The point is not that our needs are never met. Instead, the point is that the needs of all of us will only be fully met by the work of Christ in each of us.

Leadership-driven, not need-centered. Needs alone do not create community; leaders do. It's not that needs are unimportant or should be left unmet, but needs are not strong enough to create and sustain a community. Those who step forward and are willing to try to do something by bringing others together are leaders, even if they have never thought of themselves that way.

One time Jesus took his original disciples on a tour of the surrounding villages. Along the way, he felt pity and compassion because the people "were confused and helpless, like sheep without a shepherd. He said to his disciples, 'The harvest is great, but the workers are few. So pray to the Lord who is in charge of the harvest; ask him to send more workers into his fields'" (Matthew 9:36-38). Immediately after that Jesus commissioned his disciples to go and be those kinds of people, and in so doing, they became leaders.

With this in mind, our focus has been on praying, identifying, recruiting, equipping, and empowering leaders. It's the leaders who will be the ones who drive and create tangible places of belonging and discipleship. It's the leaders who ensure that God's Word is woven into the group. By God's grace, we now have hundreds of leaders who are creating groups of belonging and discipleship for a majestic mosaic of people. Some, not all, of the groups are centered on meeting a particular need or cause—homelessness, at-risk children, combating human trafficking, and so on. However, the reality is that without the leader, the need would be left unmet and the group would not exist. The need is not enough to create a group. That requires a person who cares enough to gather people and do something about it. The moment a person does that is the moment he or she has become a leader.

Open, not closed. This can be one of the harder guideposts for us to embrace, because we can worry that the next person who comes into the group is going to mess the whole thing up. I often wonder why that is. Paul gives us the secret to combating this tendency: "Don't forget that you . . . used to be outsiders. . . . You lived in this world without God and without hope" (Ephesians 2:11-12). He goes on to assure us that "because of Christ and our faith in him, we can now come boldly and confidently into God's presence" (Ephesians 3:12). Having been welcomed by God in Christ, we become welcomers.

One of my friends shared with me just what this openness looks like not only in the group he is part of but also in his life.

> I met Carlos in one of the yearlong programs called a "fellowship" that I oversee for physicians at the medical school where I teach. Carlos was my "fellow" and I guess you could say we "fellowshiped" for a year as a special friendship grew. I had lunch with Carlos's family, visited his medical practice, and spoke with his office staff. As the end of the year grew near, I recognized that we would lose the required meeting that kept us together. I wondered what would happen when the fellowship ended.
>
> One morning, I awoke with an idea; I took a risk. I decided to invite Carlos to a men's small group here at the church. More than even that, this began a routine of dinner with his family on Tuesday evenings before the group, which has continued the past two years. I have become one of the family. We look forward to our time together each week. Carlos is not quite a believer. He is not sure about all this Jesus stuff. He says he believes in a higher power but is unwilling at this point to commit to Jesus as

his Savior and only hope of salvation. I am not sure
when and if Carlos will give his life to Jesus Christ,
but I do know this: both Carlos and his family
report a transformation of some kind beginning in
his life. Our men's group has embraced Carlos with
a love that has startled him.[3]

There are lots of different ways to express openness as a small
group. Some have a permanently open door allowing anyone to come any week. Others might be open until they
start a certain study, when they close until the completion of
the study to reopen before the next study begins. Still other
groups express openness by sending out new leaders to start
new groups, welcoming in new people. *How* you do it is less
important than *that* you do it. If Jesus had stuck with a closed
group, then you and I would never have heard the good news
of the gospel.

Outward, not inward alone. Mission often has the power
to create a deep sense of joyful community. When people come
together to work toward a common goal, community is often
the by-product in a special way. Dorothy Sayers, a renowned
English essayist, wrote this right after World War II:

During World War II, one of the great surprises we
had in our lives is that we found ourselves for the
very first time happy. Why? Because for the first time
in our lives, we found ourselves doing something,

not for the pay and not for the social standing, but
for the sake of working together to get something
done that benefited everyone.[4]

Answering the community question must couple a sense
of mission with belonging. As Christians, we exist to serve
something greater than just ourselves. When Jesus invites
people to follow him, he says, "Come, follow me, and I will
show you how to fish for people!" (Matthew 4:19). "Come,
follow" creates a sense of belonging; "fish for people" creates
a sense of mission. When the two are brought together, community means that good not only happens *to* people, but also
through people.

Answering the Community Question

The moment we decide that we desire to follow Jesus, we are
confronted with an implicit question of community. It's not
just that we follow Jesus individually, but that he invites us to
follow him as part of his new redemptive community. Your
answer to what will be the marks of this community may
not be the exact same as those listed above. That's okay. God
will help you answer the question in a way that leads you to
a passionate picture of life done well together.

We were created for community. But it's more than that.
We were created for a particular kind of community, one
where we can know and be known, learn to grow in our
discipleship in Christ, and then live that out together in real

and tangible everyday ways. What will it take for that kind of community to become a regular part of your life? Or if you are already part of such a community, what is God inviting you to do to sustain that community and encourage it? However you answer the question of community, make certain that you do. Otherwise, don't be surprised if you feel drawn to start chatting with a volleyball named Wilson.

Questions Worth Being Curious About

1. Are you involved in a Christ-centered community? Why or why not? If you are not, prayerfully ask God to help you discover what is keeping you from that and what to do about it.

2. Of the six guideposts (DR GLOO), was there one that you either strongly agreed with or strongly disagreed with? Why is that? Is God revealing anything to you through those feelings?

3. God desires for us to be in his redemptive community. If you are already involved in such a community, is there anything God is asking you to do to strengthen it? Is there anyone who comes to mind for you to invite into your community?

THE MULTI-ETHNIC QUESTION: WHAT ARE WE GOING TO DO, ART?

The one who asks questions does not lose his way.

AFRICAN PROVERB

Far better an approximate answer to the right question, which is often vague, than an exact answer to the wrong question, which can always be made precise.

JOHN TUKEY

THE CHURCH THAT I SERVE is now named Christian Assembly, but that was not always its name. The story of how our name changed is one of my favorite stories of the history of our church. Here's what happened.

Our church grew out of the Azusa Street Revival, a spiritual phenomenon in Los Angeles in the early 1900s. Three twentysomething Italian women went to see what was happening at the revival and were so touched by God that they decided to start a home Bible study. That Bible study grew into a church and eventually needed a name. It was meeting in a neighborhood of mostly Italian-speaking people, and led by an Italian shoe cobbler named Arnold Bellesi. They decided to call the church the Italian Christian Assembly.

The Italian Christian Assembly was the name of our church for close to sixty-five years. But along the way, Arnold noticed that the neighborhood was changing to include more English-speaking people, so he invited a young college intern, Don Pickerill, to begin to preach in English. Don became the pastor when Arnold retired, and it's Don who tells the story of how our name changed:

> I got a phone call. "Is it permissible to attend your church?"
>
> "What do you mean?" I asked.
>
> "Well," they replied, "we are not Italians."
>
> I was caught off guard. "Whoa! Of course, we welcome anybody and everybody."

In those days, the church had a little white bus with the words "Italian Christian Assembly" printed on the side. Don took his problem to Art Botta, the bus driver. "What are we going to do, Art? People think we welcome only Italians."

Art himself was Italian. He responded, "I'll fix that."

Don finishes the story. "That day Art went to the store and bought a can of white paint and painted over the word *Italian*. So we just dropped *Italian* altogether and went by the name 'Christian Assembly' from that point forward."

I never met Art Botta. He lived before my time. However, if he could come visit Christian Assembly today, he would encounter a community of thousands of people of almost every ethnicity imaginable. Amazing what God can do with a can of paint and the right kind of heart. If Art could see it today, I think it would make his heart sing. I know it makes God's heart sing.

Antioch Again

We are not the first people to live within an increasingly multi-ethnic culture, so we can take a look back to learn some things about how to live into a multi-ethnic reality. The book of Acts introduces us to a city in the Roman Empire known as Antioch. This city was the third largest in the entire empire and was known for its vibrant intellectual life, bustling commerce, religious pluralism, and most of all, ethnic diversity. Into this setting, some nameless Jewish followers of Jesus began to share the good news of Jesus Christ with Gentiles (non-Jewish people).

The Greek word translated "Gentile" (or sometimes "nations") is *ethnos*, which is the root where we get our English word *ethnicity*. The gospel applying to multiple ethnicities is not a new thing. It's been God's plan all along. Because of that we can be confident that he is interested in helping us answer the multi-ethnic question in real and tangible ways—just like he did in Antioch.

Antioch was divided along ethnic, economic, and political lines. Literally. The ethnic divisions were so intense that Antioch actually walled off the dominant ethnic groups of its population into different quadrants. There were Greek,

Syrian, African, and Jewish sections to the city, each separated by walls. These divisions were accepted as the norm in the city around them, but the church in Antioch saw these walls as barriers to overcome, not a status quo to be maintained. Part of the unspoken witness to the authority of the Cross and the goodness of the gospel of Jesus was that people of diverse backgrounds did not hate each other or even just tolerate each other; they grew to love one another.

The leadership of those involved with the church in Antioch was a cross section of people reflecting unity without uniformity. Barnabas was a Jew, but he adopted Greek customs of language and culture. Simeon and Lucius were from two different parts of Africa. Manaen was from a wealthy, well-connected family. Paul was a Roman citizen, as well as a Jew with rabbinical training. It's a compelling picture: an increasingly diverse community who did life together in the middle of a city that walled off its people into different sections. This countercultural church lived out the tangible effects of the gospel of Jesus in everyday life.

Just as important as the church's success in overcoming these barriers and walls was the way in which they were overcome. No strategic program was established. Instead, the church's leaders preached the centrality of the Cross and the lordship of Jesus Christ for all people, and demonstrated the power of the Lord among them. When Barnabas first visited the church in Antioch, we are told, "he arrived and saw what the grace of God had done" (Acts 11:23, NIV). God's grace is the only thing powerful enough to build a multi-ethnic community of love in the midst of fear, division, or suspicion.

We are told that the disciples were first called Christians at Antioch (see Acts 11:21-26). Why is that? Standard ethnic designations of Jew, Greek, Syrian, or African no longer captured the rise of this new reality, because the only thing they held in common was Jesus Christ. In Antioch, Christians lived out the reality that the gospel that unites is stronger than the things that divide us.

The No-Romance Zone

The moment you try to answer the multi-ethnic question, you will find that it requires a lot of humility, learning, listening to others who are different from you, and regular course correction even in the best cases. The most honest version of the story is that the church has quite a mixed track record on this. We should expect nothing less, because that's how it was in the early church as well.

When it comes to the gospel and multi-ethnicity, we cannot allow ourselves to slip into a romanticized and naive version of the early church. At one point in Jerusalem, the early church instituted a distribution of food; it broke down along ethnic lines and had to be corrected. Similarly, the apostle Peter, who early on has a vision from God that opens the gospel (and ultimately the church) to Gentiles, later reverts to refusing to eat with Gentiles, and the apostle Paul has to confront him.

If we naively think the early church answered the multi-ethnic question without issues, conflicts, repentance, forgiveness, and course corrections, then we will be severely disappointed when such things arise for us in our attempts to live out a gospel for all people. If we understand, however, that the multi-ethnic question was not easily answered by the early church, then we are better prepared for challenges that arise today. We will consider such challenges part of the process of moving toward God's plan: good news for all ethnicities.

Practical Steps for Practicing Multi-Ethnicity

One of my friends is a doctor who speaks about "practicing medicine." I would imagine it's not a very comforting phrase if you are one of his patients, but at least it's honest. His idea is that while there are some things in medicine that are easy to handle—the diagnosis and prescriptions are well known, and it's an open-and-shut case—some conditions are treated through experimentation based on best guesses of the leading science at the time.

Answering the multi-ethnic question is like that. We just have to keep practicing, humbly asking the Lord to help us learn. Here are some of the questions that I and a few other people are prayerfully asking.

How does my ethnicity shape my view of the world? Part of being question-led is the fundamental recognition that you do not know everything. It's not an easy place to get to, but if you can get used to your pride taking a bit of beating, it's very freeing.

I was in a meeting a number of years ago with a couple of leaders within our church that I respect. We were discussing how to continue to develop leaders from the variety of ethnic communities represented in our church. During the conversation, I said, "At some point in the game, people who are leaders have to step up and try to lead well. That's what makes them leaders."

One of my Korean-American friends responded, "Tom, that is such a white way to view leadership." Fair enough; I am white, after all. She explained that people in Asian cultures do not necessarily self-identify as leaders; they don't jump to the front of the line to lead. Instead, they wait until someone older who is already in leadership identifies them; this serves as a sign that their elders and the community value their leadership capacity. As I have discussed this with other Asian-American leaders I know, I've found that most of them (though not all) agree with her broad-brush assessment.

It's a good thing when someone points out your naiveté—especially if you trust them enough to not feel attacked, which can lead to your dismissing their view. God used that conversation to change the way I seek to identify and encourage leaders from an Asian-American background. But more than that, how I relate to a wide variety of ethnicities on the topic of leadership was changed. Often people either do not want to discuss the multi-ethnicity question, or they pronounce themselves experts on the topic. Being a curious, question-led person is a wise course of action when it comes to understanding the dynamics of the multi-ethnic question. There is no one-size-fits-all answer, which is part of the power of asking the right questions. The early church constantly had to make course adjustments to answer the multi-ethnic question in their context, and so will we today.

How much emphasis should I place on my ethnicity if I am in Christ? Eugene Peterson once penned an article titled, "Teach Us to Care and Not to Care." Essentially he argued that caring about everything all the time is great—until you actually try to live out of your concern. Eventually, you will wind up caring about nothing none of the time. The challenge for us is to live in the tension between caring too much and not caring at all. The question is, How do we live within that tension?

Peterson was not specifically addressing ethnicity, but the multi-ethnic question lends itself to the challenge of living in tension. Art Botta was proud of his Italian ethnicity, but he cared more about the gospel of Jesus. So he set aside his ethnic heritage for the greater good of bringing the good news to people of a wide variety of ethnicities.

When we come to Christ, we do not lose our ethnicity. The Scriptures tell us that people of every tribe, tongue, and nation gather around the throne of God. That is part of the grandeur and beauty of God's Kingdom. Jesus prayed that all of his followers would be one, not the same. Diversity within the body of Christ is an essential part of its majestic beauty.

At the same time, in Christ, our identity must never be reduced to only an ethnic background. Two years ago I was invited to go to Mongolia to spend some time with believers in that country. I invited three other leaders to join me. As part of getting acclimated to the culture, one of the people with me asked one of Mongolia's key leaders questions about his country's interlacing history with China and Russia. It was a fascinating conversation; we were genuinely curious about his experience.

It's helpful to note that the word "curious" comes from the Latin word *cura*, which means "to care." When we care about someone, we ask them questions, and we listen.

At one point, my friend asked our Mongolian host, "How do you think of yourself in who you are?" Because we had been talking about the country's cultural and ethnic history, I was expecting an answer based on culture or ethnicity. What I heard instead was one of the most memorable moments of the trip. The Mongolian leader said, "How do I understand myself? Who am I? I am a beloved child of God who is a follower of Christ, seeking to learn his ways and do his will." He was not demoting his cultural and ethnic background, but his identity was not singularly conflated with it either.[1]

What questions do you wish that I was asking? The neighborhood where Christian Assembly is situated is one of the most diverse in Los Angeles (currently 40 percent Latino, 30 percent white, 24 percent Asian, 2 percent black, and 4 percent "other").[2] This presents us with plenty of opportunities to work with people from a variety of ethnicities. Of course, not every neighborhood will be as diverse as ours. Nevertheless, asking our way to the world God wants in the area of multi-ethnicity often includes being curious about where and how you can build relationships of trust with people of various ethnic backgrounds. In some cases it may mean being intentional about pursuing relationships outside your mono-ethnic neighborhood—whether that takes you across the city or across the world.

One of our efforts in Los Angeles is to bring local churches together to plant gospel-centered churches. One of the beauties of this is that it has allowed natural learning relationships to develop between leaders of a variety of ethnicities. As the relationships develop, so does the trust to have increasingly curious and honest conversations, each of us open to the fact that God might use other leaders to teach us something. This level of engagement has resulted in some of my closest friendships being with people of different ethnic backgrounds—different from me, but also different from one another. A few of these relationships have developed enough trust over the years that now I ask these brothers and sisters in Christ, "What questions do you wish I was asking you?"

We do not have it all figured out by any means. That's

the whole point. Being curious means recognizing that you don't have it all figured out, trusting God to lead you through questions into the world God wants. Just as the early church had to constantly course correct together, we don't expect to figure everything out. But we do know that God's final goal is not a mono-ethnic kingdom, but the gospel for all the ethnicities.

A Question Full of Care

"What are we going to do, Art?" It was a question that demonstrated care for those who were not Italian but wanted to follow Christ. The Italian Christian Assembly was curious because they cared, and the questions that arose set the stage for a whole new future. Had they stayed the Italian Christian Assembly, the church would have slowly declined as the neighborhood changed. Instead, God used that curiosity born of care to set the stage for a truly multi-ethnic church of several thousands.

The multi-ethnic question is not a simple question with a simple answer. It clearly does not have one single answer. It's the type of question that we have to humbly stumble through with the conviction that God is honored by our efforts. In the Bible, we are given a picture of heaven that includes

> a great multitude that no one could count, from
> every nation, tribe, people and language, standing

before the throne and before the Lamb. . . . And they
cried out in a loud voice:

"Salvation belongs to our God,
who sits on the throne,
and to the Lamb."

REVELATION 7:9-10, NIV

It's a powerful picture of a unified, not uniform people. We
are united by the gospel of the one who prayed that his followers, though not the same, would be one. Because people
from every tribe, tongue, and nation matter to God, they
matter to us, increasingly as we seek to know God and trust
his plans. And because relationships across ethnic lines are
part of God's Kingdom vision, we can pursue them with
confidence that our lives will be richer and better for them.

Questions Worth Being Curious About

1. Have you ever felt misunderstood by someone of a
   different ethnicity? How did you handle those feelings?
   Are you able to bring those feelings to God? Why or
   why not? Were you able to work through the issue with
   that person? Why or why not? Would you want to if it
   were possible?

2. Do you have anyone in your life of a different ethnicity
   that you trust and respect enough to ask what they
   wish you would ask them? If not, what can you do to

cultivate that? If so, are you willing to ask them those questions and simply listen? Why or why not?

3. The Bible tells us that God is gathering people of every tribe, tongue, and nation into his Kingdom. How does that make you feel? Why do you think you feel that way? If you feel excited by that, prayerfully ask God what step he is asking you to take to live into that reality now.

10

THE MULTI-GENERATIONAL QUESTION: HAS THE GOSPEL LOST ITS POWER WITH THE NEXT GENERATION?

The quality of a leader cannot be judged by the
answer he gives, but by the questions he asks.

SIMON SINEK

To what can I compare this generation? . . . How can I describe them?

JESUS, IN LUKE 7:31

WORLD-FAMOUS TENOR LUCIANO PAVAROTTI once told about an encounter with his father that deeply marked his life. "When I was a boy," he said, "my father, a baker, introduced me to the wonders of song. He urged me to work very hard to develop my voice. Arrigo Pola, a professional tenor in my hometown of Modena, Italy, took me as a pupil. . . . However, I also enrolled in a teachers' college. On graduating, I asked my father, 'Should I be a teacher or a singer?'"

His father told him, "Luciano, if you try to sit on two chairs, you will fall between them. For life, you must choose one chair and be singularly devoted to that one chair."

Luciano chose song. His first professional performance

would not come for seven years—with another seven before he performed at the Metropolitan Opera. "Now," he later reflected, "I think whether it's laying bricks, writing a book—whatever we choose—we should give ourselves to it."[1]

Luciano began his vocational life unsettled about which "chair" he would give himself to throughout his life. Only once he settled on his "chair" did he begin to live into what mattered to him. If we believe the gospel is a gospel for each generation—a multi-generational gospel so to speak—then one of the questions that we must settle is whether, as some evidence may seem to suggest, the gospel has lost its power with the young adult generation. And if not, how can we live into the reality of a multi-generational gospel here and now?

The response to the gospel is growing significantly around much of the globe, but not necessarily in the United States. Membership in the country's largest Christian denomination is expected to fall by 50 percent by 2050, unless the aging denomination reverses a fifty-year trend and does more to reach out to young adults.[2]

We cannot be confused, unclear, or uncommitted in our answer to the multi-generational question. As it's been said, "The church is always only one generation away from extinction."[3] Either we think the gospel will flourish only with certain generations or certain life stages, or we believe it has the power to touch people of every generation and all stages of life. If it has the power to touch people of every generation, then we need to figure out how to turn that from words to reality.

God, the Gospel, and 108 Years of Next Generations

God is a multi-generational God. A quick scan of the Bible shows this repeatedly. He tells Noah that the rainbow is a sign for all generations to come (Genesis 9:12). He tells Moses that he is the God of Abraham, Isaac, and Jacob—in other words, the God of multiple generations (Exodus 3:6). He tells Moses to tell the people that God's name is to be remembered for all generations (Exodus 3:15). When the people are fed in the wilderness by manna, God commands that two quarts of manna be kept in a container so that future generations will see it (Exodus 16:32-33). The Psalms tell us that God's faithfulness continues to each generation, and his fame endures to every generation (Psalms 100:5; 102:12). God is clear: He is not a single-generation God. When we reach out to the next generation, we are joining God in his goal and plan. Not every person in any generation will respond to the gospel, but God has people in every generation and is on the side of those who want to make a place for the next generation to know him and find life in his Word and ways. That's hopeful news for us to remember.

Wrestling with the question of the gospel reaching the next generation is not a new thing. It's been going on for thousands of years. Christian Assembly began in 1907; since then the question has led us to try all sorts of ways of reaching and enfolding young adults among the other generations. From our genesis, young adults have been a core part of the community. In fact, the church was started by three young adults who had an encounter with God. One hundred and eight years later, it's a remarkable thing to be part of a church that has as many young adults as ever alongside all the other generations. When I am asked why that is the case, here is what I tell them.

From Generation to Generation

Everyone has a "next generation." No matter what age you are right now, there is someone who is younger than you. By the time you finish reading this sentence, there will be even more people who are younger than you. We are all the older generation to someone.

The younger generation is responsible *to* the older generation, but the older generation is responsible *for* the younger generation. One leader put it this way: "When the Kingdom of God is working right, the generations get stronger."[4] As I remind our young adults, they also have a next generation—the students. As we remind our students, they also have a next generation—the elementary school children. Certainly, the largest responsibility for children falls to the parents, but here again, we see the principle that the older generation has a role and a responsibility for the success of the next generation knowing God and following him wholeheartedly.

Regularly we remind Christian Assembly that we stand on the shoulders of those who went before us, praying for this day and for this generation. Likewise, we need to be praying for each rising generation.

The way it is supposed to work is that each generation tells of God's faithfulness to the next (Isaiah 38:19). Dozens and dozens of times the Bible speaks of remembrances of the good things God has done being passed from "generation to generation."[5] This is to be done so that "each generation should set its hope anew on God" (Psalm 78:7). The onus is always on older generations to find ways to help younger generations thrive in faith in God. So how do we do that?

The first question we ask is, *how can we create space for each generation*? Every generation needs not just a place to attend but also a people to be part of. This requires both acknowledging and adapting to the needs of the younger generation. Again, older generations are responsible for younger generations. For example, we spent an entire weekend teaching on singleness. Singleness is not solely a young adult issue—not by any means in Los Angeles—but speaking so intentionally to it helps young adults know that their concerns and realities are being acknowledged and considered.

While it's common for young adults to be under-represented in churches, here in Los Angeles there are churches that are filled almost exclusively with young adults. One of my friends leads one of them; he rightly recognizes that a mono-generational church does not reflect the multi-generational heart of God, and so his questions center on how to create space for older people.

Creating space for each generation includes not only creating spaces of belonging and teaching to their realities, but also making space for their leadership, with genuine decision-making responsibilities. It includes making them visible in the life of the church, including at weekend services. The single largest factor in young adults feeling welcome at a church is whether they see other young adults in leadership. Two of our largest ongoing local outreach efforts for the poor and at-risk were started and led by people in their twenties. This sounds easy but can actually be quite hard to do, because it requires sacrifices on everyone's part. The rising generation, for example, may not want to do things the way they have been done. This can surface feelings of insecurity in the older generations as changes are suggested. Moreover, a younger generation might be prone to leadership mistakes that more seasoned people would see and avoid. That is part of the price tag of creating space for the next generation.

Young adults who are part of a multi-generational community must also, however, make space for those preferences of an older generation. What is the right balance? That is an answer that is discovered and lived out one day at a time. That's why you have to be rock-solid certain that God is interested in a multi-generational church. Each person has to ask if they care more about their preferences, or about being part of a multi-generational church.

It goes even further than that. If we do care mainly about our preferences, how do we square that with a life of faith, where we are often asked to sacrifice and trust? When decisions seem to be driven by the preferences of one generation, whether younger or older, that generation will define the church, and the church will fall short in its mission.

The second thing we ask is, *how can each generation create time for one another?* In our case, we have found it curious that older adults can feel as though young adults do not want or value time with them, when the reality is the exact opposite. Many young adults are looking for someone to mentor them, to invest in them, to create time for them. Of course, some of this can be driven by narcissism, but that's not often the case. Usually, young adults are navigating weighty decisions—schooling, careers, living situations, marriages, children, and more—and want someone to help them see life with a bit of perspective.

To me, the most inspiring people in our church are not simply those who live faithful lives, but who also make the time to equip the next generation to do the same. For example, we have businesspeople who have intentionally identified young adults in business to talk with about how the gospel helps them engage in business differently. We have parents who help young adults discover proven ways to raise children with a heart for God. We have married couples who have been through many ups and downs who now are walking with newly married young adult couples. The list could go on, and thankfully the same applies to many other churches.

The third question that guides us is, *how can we create wins for each generation?* It's not enough to simply *celebrate* the wins of a specific age group. You have to be part of *creating* them. Consider the tribes of Reuben and Gad, and the half-tribe of Manasseh. They settled on the east side of the Jordan River, rather than going further with the rest of Israel into the Promised Land. Things were good for them there; they were "ahead" of other tribes in the sense that they already had their land. But then Joshua challenged them:

> Your strong warriors, fully armed, must lead the other tribes across the Jordan to help them conquer their territory. Stay with them until the LORD gives them rest, as he has given you rest, and until they, too, possess the land the LORD your God is giving them.
>
> JOSHUA 1:14-15

This is not a story from one generation to another, but rather from one tribe to another, and yet the principle is instructive. It's not enough to wish, want, or pray for another generation to know God and live in ways that honor God and help them thrive. We are responsible to be part of *creating the wins* for them wherever it's within our power to do so.

The final question that guides us is, *how can we create courage in each generation?* The other three items are things we do *for* the each generation. This is a question about what we can do *in* them. As we work hard to create space, time, and wins for each generation at Christian Assembly, we realize that each generation will need to move forward to what

God is asking of them without relinquishing those opportunities to fear or insecurity. In other words, they need courage. The points of fear that face a young adult will probably be different from those of an older or even the oldest generation, but each generation has fears that must be combated as we move through the stages of life.

The way that God most often gives us courage is by surrounding us with a community of encouragement across generations. For example, for young adults the best kind of encouragement comes from an older generation who welcomes them, loves them, believes in them, and helps them steer through the ups and downs of life. What has been interesting to see is how encouraged the older generations are when they see the younger generations knowing Christ and finding joy in following him courageously. It's like encouragement is contagious.

Something Only God Can Help Us Answer

When I first joined the Christian Assembly pastoral team, my focus was to lead young adults to complete commitment to Christ. As part of that, I thought it would be great to establish what I called "grandparents in the faith." So I did a bit of "social engineering." I selected ten twentysomethings and ten seniors to have lunch together. I explained that I thought this could be the beginning of a great answer to the multi-generational question.

It was a very bad answer to a very good question.

After I shared about God being a multi-generational God and wanting a multi-generational church, we shared a meal together. I knew things were headed in the wrong direction when one of the older gentlemen asked why one of the younger guys had an earring. His tone was less than curious. One of the older women commented that she did not approve of all the tattoos on the young adults around the table. The responses from a couple of young adults were no more helpful. Let's just say we did not do any more "grandparents in the faith" lunches.

And yet, the question still remained. We just had to live into different answers. In time that has happened, but we have found that programs alone cannot answer this question. It's a process of quietly and constantly cultivating love between generations, one relationship at a time.

The gospel has not lost its power with the next generation. More often, local churches are too slow to adapt the nonessentials in their church—those matters that don't compromise the gospel message—to address the needs of rising generations. The reality is that if there is a missing generation in many local churches, it is most often young adults.

We all must be unequivocal in our commitment to building a home for all the generations. We do this because it is God's heart. He is the one who goes out looking for what is lost or missing, and he invites us to join him.

You can do this by asking how you can create more time, space, and wins *for* other people of other generations. Then we all must create courage *in* each generation to move toward what God is inviting them to be and do.

The good news is we can stand confident of God's Word that his salvation will continue from generation to generation (Isaiah 51:8). May God give us the conviction to sit on one chair: the conviction that God's heart is for every generation *and* for a multi-generational people. From there the question becomes how to live into that reality right where we are, in our neighborhoods and in our relational networks. I do not know how God will lead you to live into the answer of that question in your life, but I do know that as we ask our way to the world God wants, it will include everyday ways where each generation sets its hope anew on God together.

Questions to Be Curious About

1. Do you think the gospel has lost its touch with young adults? Why or why not? If you think the gospel is for all the generations, how do you account for the fact that young adults are underrepresented in many local churches?

2. What preferences are you willing to sacrifice to make space for a different generation in your church?

3. Consider your relational network. How many of them are part of a different generation? How can you create time, space, and wins for someone of a different

generation? Does doing that excite you or not? Why or why not?

4. If you are connected to a local church, is it multi-generational? Is there any generation that is underrepresented? Why is that? Is there anything that you prayerfully sense God inviting you to do to help your local church become even more multi-generational?

11

THE LOCAL QUESTION: IF OUR CHURCH MOVED OUT OF THE NEIGHBORHOOD, WOULD ANYONE CARE?

Life's most persistent and urgent question is,
"What are you doing for others?"
DR. MARTIN LUTHER KING JR.

Which of these three would you say was a neighbor?
JESUS, IN LUKE 10:36

A NUMBER OF YEARS AGO, things were going well at Christian Assembly. We had just celebrated our one-hundred-year birthday. Most things that are a hundred years old are dead or close to it, but by the grace of God, Christian Assembly was in the midst of some of its best years on record: Attendance and giving were up; we had just paid off all the buildings, becoming debt free; people were coming to know Christ on a regular basis; there was an energy in our times of worship; and people genuinely seemed excited to be part of the church.

It was just about that time that we began to ask this question, first among our leadership team, but then with the church as a whole: If everyone who attends this church moved out of the neighborhood, would anyone outside this church care? Things were great for Christian Assembly, but was Christian Assembly great for the neighborhood?

This is a question that every leader needs to ask. It will change your "organizational scorecard," so to speak. It's one thing to mean something to those who belong to the church; it's quite another challenge to mean something to those who do not. I felt like we had the right question, but apart from feeling like we were striking out, I had no idea how to begin to matter to those outside of our church in a real and ongoing way. But asking that question often and openly is the key to unleashing some of the most creative and enduring answers.

Christian Assembly is centered in a great neighborhood of Los Angeles called Eagle Rock. It was recently named the "second hottest neighborhood" in the country by a national real estate firm.[1] It has incredible places to eat, and you can meet people from every walk of life here. It is salt-of-the-earth, one of the most ethnically diverse neighborhoods in one of the most ethnically diverse cities in the country.[2]

For all that is great about Eagle Rock, like any neighborhood, it's not without challenges. More than half of the kids in our closest elementary school are on a free or reduced-price lunch program. The night after my wife and I first moved into the neighborhood, someone was shot two blocks away. On another occasion, I walked home from work and came across a three-on-one street fight. Let's just say that can make for a less than fun walk. Once, when we offered "free prayer" in front of a local store, one of toughest looking guys you can imagine asked us to pray: That night he was scheduled to literally fight his way out of a gang.

What does it look like to be good news in that kind of setting? We did not know, but we did know that Jesus was once asked a question that led to a story about being a neighbor that matters. Apparently, if you follow Jesus long enough, he will lead you into the neighborhood. And even more, your neighborhood apparently has something to do with eternal life.

A Question Answered with a Neighborhood Story

One day a teacher of religious law asks Jesus this question: "What must I do to inherit eternal life?" (literally, "the life of the ages"; see Luke 10:25-37, NIV).

Jesus responds to the question with—you guessed it— a question. "What does the law of Moses say?"

The man answers, "'You must love the LORD your God with all your heart, all your soul, all your strength, and all your mind.' And, 'Love your neighbor as yourself.'"

Jesus affirms him. "Right! Do this and you will live!"

But wanting to justify himself, the man asked a follow-up: "And who is my neighbor?"

So Jesus tells a neighborhood story. "A Jewish man was traveling from Jerusalem down to Jericho."

The people listening knew this road well. It was narrow, full of twists and turns, and had a desert on either side of it. It was easy for thieves to slip in from the desert, assault and rob someone, and then disappear back into the desert. Even today, the road is known as the "Red and Bloody Way" because so much violence has occurred there.

Jesus tells of a man who has been robbed and left there, beaten and half-dead. Three familiar figures also happen to be traveling on the road. The first is a priest, who would have been the top of the religious leadership food chain. The second is a Levite, one step below a priest. Both of these two are entrusted with worship and keeping the traditions of Israel alive; both of them pass by the injured man without stopping to help.

The third person coming by the helpless, half-dead man is identified as a Samaritan. It helps us to know that Samaritans practiced a heretical version of Judaism, they were ethnically distinct from the Jews, and most Jews from that day would not have expected anything loving or heroic from a Samaritan. But as Jesus' story continues, the Samaritan stops, gets off his donkey, and does what he can to help the man. He takes him to the nearest inn, where the wounded man will receive long-term care, and he pays for all of this out of his own pocket.

The man had asked Jesus, "Who is my neighbor?" and Jesus' story is focused on setting up Jesus' question back to the man: "Which of these three would you say was a neighbor to the man?"

The answer is obvious right? The one who showed mercy. Jesus then tells the man, "Go and do likewise."

Did you catch what Jesus did by asking that question?

People in Jesus' day looked for ways to limit their moral and ethical responsibilities to others. There were debates about what the term *neighbor* meant, constantly reducing its meaning to tighter and narrower definitions. People wanted to do the minimum amount of work to be considered loving, and not an ounce more. That seems silly to read about, but I can find those same tendencies in my own heart, living in a world with such nonstop overwhelming needs.

By the end of the story, Jesus has turned the question inside out. "Who is my neighbor?" now has become "What kind of neighbor will I be?"

What started as a discussion about the nature of other people, about what kind of person was worthy of love, has now become a question about what kind of person we will become. If our identity is genuinely that we are beloved of God, then our character, our deepest impulse is to love others—not because they are worthy of love, or because we want them to thank us, or to increase the attendance in the weekend worship services—but because God first loved us.

Asking Questions, Living Answers

So let's go back to modern-day Los Angeles. Our question was still on the table: If we all left the neighborhood, would anyone who does not attend our church care? In other words, will we be the kind of neighbors that leave others better off than when we first met them? Can we become the kind of people who are good for the neighborhood? We knew that the point of the story was Jesus' invitation to become that kind of neighbor, that kind of person.

Sometimes God asks us a question not because he wants us to answer it, but because he wants us to begin to live it. That's what happened as we asked this question together. I could tell you dozens of stories of how people began to live into the answers to that question, but let me offer you just two. In them, I hope you will see how being question-led can lead to things that none of us first imagined would or could happen.

For the good of the neighborhood: Sarah's story. When I first met Sarah, she was a twentysomething who had become part of Christian Assembly. A former art teacher, she had moved to Los Angeles to make it in acting. As is often the case, things had not worked out exactly as she had hoped. To make ends meet, she was driving a lettuce truck, working at farmer's markets. It happens to be a great way to be with a lot of people in the neighborhood.

Over time, Sarah became more involved in the life of the church. As part of that, she was exposed to the local question we were asking. Sarah and I met monthly for a year to talk about leadership, to wrestle with questions, and to discern what might be her next steps. As it happens, Sarah has a heart for at-risk kids. Part of that comes from her own life: She could have been classified as an at-risk child. As she prayed and researched, she came across Kids Hope (www.kidshopeusa.org), an organization that mobilizes people to mentor at-risk children in their neighborhood via the local church.

Sarah approached the principal at our local public elementary school about starting a mentoring and tutoring program for at-risk kids. Sarah would mentor a child and invite and coach others from our church to do the same. Each mentor would spend one hour a week with a child, working on whatever the local teachers felt was needed. We began with a handful of kids, and as with any new thing, there were questions that were asked and suspicions that had to be overcome. We even had to promise one family that we would never mentor their child.

Seven years later, we have about eighty kids being mentored by members of Christian Assembly on a weekly basis. It's making a difference in their test scores at school and in their lives. Not only that, but other kids are taking notice of the changes as well. In fact, Sarah recently showed me a collection of notes she has received from kids in the school who would like a mentor. One of the most poignant came from a little girl who could not remember the word *mentor*; her note simply asked, "Dear Ms. Sarah, Can you give me a hope too?"

Sarah noted, "I think kids all over this city are asking that question." It's a question worth being curious about, a question worthy of an answer we live into.

Sarah's initiative is not just making a difference in kids' lives; it's making a difference in adult lives as well. The mentors are not just hearing good news on the weekends at our gatherings; they are *being* good news during the week and impacting the staff of the school. In fact, at one point, the principal said,

"I am not a Christian. I do not believe in God. But if I ever do believe in a god, I will believe in their God, because their God makes life better for the most at-risk kids in my school."

Similarly, after years of observing the mentoring program, the family that was most resistant to our efforts has now decided that they are in favor of our efforts. Loving our neighbor consistently over time has the power to overcome the deepest suspicions.

Our leadership team never had some strategic vision to launch a mentoring program. We simply felt like we had a question that might lead us to live into an answer. In fact, it has not just led us. Other local church leaders are taking notice, and some have begun their own Kids Hope effort at their local elementary school. At this point, literally hundreds of at-risk kids are being given a chance and hope because of how a former at-risk kid was led to discover a way to live into an answer to the local question.

Good for 119 neighborhoods: Kevin's story. Kevin is not part of Christian Assembly. He is a former attorney-turned-church-planter who launched a church in downtown Los Angeles. He believes the local church is meant to both be and declare good news, and he felt downtown Los Angeles was a good place to do that.

Kevin and I met a couple of years ago at the insistence of a few mutual friends. If you met him, you'd like him. He's smart, humble, easygoing, but committed to Christ and the work he feels assigned to do.

Kevin was the key person to help Christian Assembly find another way to live into the answer to the local impact question. The idea was this: There are 119 neighborhoods in the official governance structure of Los Angeles as a city. What if we were able to start communities of Jesus in every neighborhood in Los Angeles?

Kevin shared a process of bringing local churches together to plant other local churches for the good of the neighborhood and the living out of the gospel in real and tangible ways. As a leadership team, we never had a strategic vision to plant a bunch of churches. And yet, as we wrestled with this question, we felt a divine sense that this was a way for us as a church to love our neighbors by creating little engines of good in each neighborhood. As we kept trying to "go and do likewise," as Jesus said, what has arisen from that effort is something called the Los Angeles Church Planting Movement (www.lacpm.org). At this point the effort is just under two years old and has gathered thirty-four churches from seventeen different denominations or affiliations.

In an increasingly shrinking globe, our neighbors can be across the street or across the world. So eventually we expanded our church-planting vision to include church plants among the global poor through a partnership with Compassion International (www.compassion.org). The idea was that starting churches among the global poor would give at-risk children in those areas the opportunity to be sponsored via Compassion to break the cycle of poverty. However, we have to be careful to not always define our neighbors as people who are far away as it absolves us from loving those who are in our everyday lives.

Since launching LACPM, fourteen churches have been planted—seven in Los Angeles and seven among the global poor. That's fourteen more communities that are asking the question of how they are being invited to love their neighborhoods because of being loved by God.

Remarkably, Sarah's story and Kevin's story came together in an unforeseen way. From the efforts of bringing local churches together to plant gospel-centered neighborhood churches, relationships have been developing among local churches that otherwise would not interact. But Christian Assembly recently had the opportunity to celebrate Easter with two other churches at the Hollywood Bowl in Los Angeles. Approximately 15,000 people came together to celebrate the good news of Jesus Christ. The cash offering from the service was given to help empower efforts serving at-risk kids in the neighborhoods of Los Angeles.

Living the End of the Story

Jesus answered the question "Who is my neighbor?" with a story that reconceived the question as "What kind of neighbor will I be?" A succinct answer that limited our responsibility to others was what motivated the original question, but Jesus' question challenges us to be merciful to others. I have no idea why the Samaritan stopped, got off his donkey, and loved his bruised neighbor. Jesus does not give us that answer. If you think about it, the whole episode ends a bit unfinished. We are never told whether the lawyer went from there and lived the love that he could quote so well. In a real sense, we are left to finish the story in our own lives.

The point is that the Samaritan did it, and so can we. If we follow in the steps of the Samaritan, then certainly our neighbors would care if we left the neighborhood. We don't need to do exactly what Sarah and Kevin did. But each of us needs to ask the question, to ourselves and those we serve, of what kind of neighbor God wants us to become. How do we contextualize the love of God consistently in tangible ways in our own neighborhood?

It's a question worth asking ourselves and also others who are followers of Christ around us. Many of your answers will include things that I could never imagine, which is part of the beauty of being question-led in life. Whatever answer you live into, it will certainly include being so compelled by mercy rooted in love that if you moved away from your neighborhood, those around you would sit up, take notice, and grieve.

Questions Worth Being Curious About

1. If your local church moved out of the neighborhood, would anyone who does not attend the church care? Why or why not?

2. What kind of neighbor do you think you are to those around you? Do you know those who live immediately near you, on your block or in your apartment? Why or why not? Is there something you can do to get to know them if you do not already?

3. What are the needs you see in your immediate neighborhood? Is there some way you can do something about one of them?

4. In a world filled with so many needs, do you believe it's possible to keep your heart full of mercy toward others? If not, why not? If so, how can that happen? Is there anywhere you feel like your heart has become calloused toward your neighbor? If so, ask God what you can do about that in prayer.

12

THE GLOBAL QUESTION: WHAT IS OUR RESPONSIBILITY TO UNREACHED PEOPLE GROUPS?

What people think of as the moment of discovery
is really the discovery of the question.

JONAS SALK

You can tell whether a man is clever by his answers.
You can tell whether a man is wise by his questions.

NAGUIB MAHFOUZ

HAVE YOU EVER TRIED to act smarter than you really are?

A nervous American student had to take an examination, which had two parts, oral and written. He did not mind the written examination, but looked forward to the oral exam with some misgivings. His friends told him it would be fatal to show any hesitancy, as the examiners would put that down to ignorance. He must give some sort of answer, or if he did not know the answer, try to give the impression that he had a good knowledge of the subject.

Entering the examination room, he was asked a question on a subject with which he was not at all familiar. Nevertheless, he put on a good face. "I'm sorry," he said.

"I have covered that ground and know the answer, but I have forgotten it for a moment."

"What a tragedy that you have forgotten it!" said the examiner. "Scientists have been searching for an answer to that question for the last two thousand years."

Jesus Answers a Question Directly

Years ago, a few of us began to ask this question: "What is our responsibility to parts of the world that have little or no access to the gospel—and what are we to do about it?" Discovering our responsibility was easy enough. Knowing exactly what to do about it has been challenging followers of Christ for two thousand years.

Ironically, our question grew out of one of Jesus' rare direct answers to a question: no question, no parable, no cryptic action, but a direct response to his disciples.

First, let's consider some of Jesus' final words to his followers, immediately prior to ascending to heaven. Mark records them simply as, "Go into all the world and preach the Good News to everyone" (Mark 16:15). Matthew goes into greater detail:

I have been given all authority in heaven and on earth. Therefore, go and make disciples of all the nations, baptizing them in the name of the Father and the Son and the Holy Spirit. Teach these new disciples to obey all the commands I have given

> you. And be sure of this: I am with you always,
> even to the end of the age.
>
> MATTHEW 28:18-20

Luke has Jesus telling us that the gospel "would be proclaimed in the authority of his name to all the nations, beginning in Jerusalem: 'There is forgiveness of sins for all who repent'" (Luke 24:47). And in the book of Acts, Luke records Jesus saying, "You will receive power when the Holy Spirit comes upon you. And you will be my witnesses, telling people about me everywhere—in Jerusalem, throughout Judea, in Samaria, and to the ends of the earth" (Acts 1:8).

One of the things that speech communicators tell you is that you want to make your most important points either at the very beginning of a talk or at the end of your time. People are most attentive at the beginning, and most likely to remember something from the end. So it's significant that Jesus ends his time with his disciples by making it clear that the gospel is for people from all the nations. He also made it clear that this mission was not just for him; it was now the mission of his followers.

Earlier, when the disciples privately asked Jesus, "What sign will signal your return and the end of the world?" Jesus' response included some cryptic remarks. But even then he emphasized that "the Good News about the Kingdom will be preached throughout the whole world, so that all nations will hear it; and then the end will come" (Matthew 24:14). Jesus is clear that the preaching of the gospel to all the nations is essential to God's redemptive plan for history. His words are clear that the Holy Spirit will empower us in this effort. However, he is also clear that those who are his followers have a real and consequential responsibility in this.

Some Good News, and Some Sobering News, About the Spread of the Good News

There is some good news to celebrate about where things stand since Jesus gave his followers the command to preach the whole gospel to the whole world. The people who study such things speak of about 24,000 people groups in the world.[1] In AD 100, there were twelve unreached people groups per local congregation of believers. Amazingly, today two thirds of the world's people groups have heard and have people from within that group who have embraced the gospel, resulting in strong local churches led by national leaders with a serious commitment to continue sharing the gospel with the rest of their own people group.[2] There are now more than 1,000 local congregations per people group that are unreached.[3] In other words, there are fewer people groups left to reach and exponentially more potential people and resources to reach them with. In fact, the New Testament has been translated into the languages of 94 percent of the world's population.[4]

With all the great news that there is on this front, there is some sobering news as well. Christians make up 33 percent of the world's population, but earn 53 percent of the world's annual income—and spend 98 percent of it on themselves.[5] It's estimated that $310 million annually goes toward the work of reaching unreached people groups[6]—$60 million *less* than what Americans spend on Halloween costumes for our pets.[7] Don't get me wrong. I like pets. I have a dog, but ouch!

For every $100,000 that Christians earn, we give $1 to share the gospel with the unreached people groups.[8] In terms of odds, 1 in 100,000 is the same chance you have of dying from lightning.[9] It is slightly more likely that your dollar will be committed to reaching the unreached than that you, over the course of your adult life, will be injured by a pogo stick.[10] I understand that there is more to the gospel than money, but Jesus himself said that where your treasure is, your heart will also be (Matthew 6:21). We often think, *If my heart gets touched, then I will give toward reaching the unreached.* Instead, Jesus seems to be saying, if you send some of your treasure to reach the unreached, then your heart will care more—be more curious—about making disciples of the nations.

A Prayerful Question on Jesus' Final Words

With all this rattling around my heart, I began to ask the global question with some of the others at Christian Assembly. We knew from Jesus' final words that we had some responsibility. And we knew that in an increasingly global culture, it was now easier than any other time in history to be involved around the globe. However, we also knew that there were linguistic challenges, countries that were closed to the gospel, and many other challenges. The question felt so complex (at least to me) that we prayed, waited, and watched.

After we spent a couple of months praying, a person in our church approached me with the question about whether we would be interested in considering expanding our mission effort to include one of the five remaining communist countries. It turns out that there are unreached people groups within this particular country. From there, we met with a man who had come to the United States as a refugee when he was a teenager; he now had a heart to see the gospel preached in the country he once fled. His idea was simply that Christian Assembly consider allowing our weekend teaching messages to be translated into the native language of his country— a country that had restricted access to the gospel.

With investment from the church's mission funds, we decided to distribute our messages through cell phones, which would not allow the government to jam the signal. (Radio signals were being jammed by the government.) I can't say too much more about that project's specifics other than to tell you that our little team did not know anything about how this could work. We simply had been praying, waiting, and watching for God to send an answer to our complex question. We knew we had a responsibility as Christians to those who had restricted or no access to the gospel, but we did not know how to move past some of the political, linguistic, and technological barriers. To me, that's the beauty of being question-led. You don't have to have all the answers. You just have to be willing to ask the right kind of questions prayerfully and then act when God opens up an opportunity.

This all happened about five years ago. Our hope at the time was that we might be able to get the content to 10,000 people. Honestly, that number seemed quite ambitious to us. We were not even certain if people on the other side of the world would be interested in messages crafted for people in Los Angeles. Nevertheless, we knew it was worth the risk to try something, and this was the something God had put in front of us. We did not know what would happen, but we were curious to at least give it a shot to find out.

We were surprised when we had 10,000 listeners. Then we were shocked when it climbed to 50,000 people. At the time of this writing, 450,000 people in a country that suppresses the gospel are hearing the gospel through messages translated into their own language.

Even as that effort was developing, we continued to pray about our global responsibility. We batted around ideas that were the best that we could think of, but God's next answer to our question was beyond what we could have planned.

In time, a different person came to us asking if we would ever be interested in being involved with the underground, persecuted church in a country with an Islamic theocratic government. The question we had been asking and praying made us prioritize the time to hear her idea. She then connected us with a few other leaders who were working in that area. They offered four action steps.

The first step was simply to pray for some of the leaders who had been put in jail for their faith in Christ.

The second step was to raise awareness of the situation in the country.

The third step was to consider giving money so that New Testaments could be distributed in the country. It cost about $5 per New Testament to print them. The organization had recently finished distributing a million New Testaments in the national language, and now needed to raise another $5 million to purchase the next million copies. Amazingly, a national official had held up the New Testament on a national media agency broadcast, telling people not to read it. As you can imagine, that led to even more people in the country wanting to get hold of this banned book.

The last action step was to consider traveling to an undisclosed location to train some of the young Christian leaders from that country.

We were able to do all four steps. Jesus had given a command that led to our question; God had answered our question in ways that we could never have dreamed up on our own.

Discovering Our Role in the Global Question

Jesus' final words to his disciples were to challenge us to take our place in ensuring that the gospel is preached to all people groups. Much has happened, and yet, there is still much to be done. Thankfully, we are not alone in this effort. The Holy Spirit will empower us as we move forward even when we can't imagine what it might look like. Likewise, God is on the move to raise up people who might have the creativity, cultural connections, and access to countries that we might not have. Jesus' words were spoken to his disciples together. It's fair to assume that means that this is something that no one person or one local church can do alone. Instead, it's a question that God will answer by bringing different parts of his people together. God has been on the move through history, and Christians now have more resources than ever to invest into reaching unreached groups.

Our responsibility as Christians is clear. What specifically can you do if you are not already involved in the global effort? Let me mention three things if you are curious:

1. Educate yourself and those you influence on the progress, opportunities, and challenges to complete the task of sharing the gospel to all the nations. There are several great resources for this. One of the best is the Joshua Project: www.joshuaproject.net.
2. Prayerfully ask God to show you what your responsibility is to the parts of the world with restricted or no access to the gospel. Then wait and watch while you pray for the people of the world. God will make a way to live an answer to your

question of how specifically he's inviting you to join him in his global mission.

3. Reorient your finances (and those of the organization you serve if you are a leader) to create space for empowering the sharing of the gospel. In our case, we did this before we even knew what opportunities God would send our way, which meant we were ready to act when the opportunity came.

Anyone who thinks they can answer exactly how God will work in and through us to bring about the preaching of the gospel to the all the nations is acting smarter than they really are. It's a huge task. But make no mistake and be encouraged: it will happen. As we are told in the Bible,

> I saw a vast crowd, too great to count, from every
> nation and tribe and people and language, standing
> in front of the throne and before the Lamb. . . .
> They were shouting with a great roar,
>
> "Salvation comes from our God who sits on the throne
> and from the Lamb!"
>
> REVELATION 7:9-10

Not only will this happen, but God is inviting us to be part of it. We do not have to know the answer to every question because God knows more than we do. Our job is to be ready to act when he invites us to begin to live out the answer.

Questions Worth Being Curious About

1. Do you think that you have any responsibility to those who have no access or restricted access to the gospel? Why or why not?

2. If you see that responsibility, have you asked God how he is inviting you to become part of that mission? Why or why not?

3. If you have prayerfully asked that question, has God surfaced anyone in your life or any thoughts that might be the beginning of a pathway to live into an answer? If so, how might you follow up moving that thought or that relationship toward a tangible action supporting the mission of sharing the gospel with all the nations?

13

THE LEGACY QUESTION: WHAT WILL MATTER IN THE END?

Judge a man by his questions rather than his answers.

VOLTAIRE

We grow up never questioning that which is unquestioned around us.

MARGARET MEAD

NOT TOO LONG AGO, something strange happened in Maine. In a quintessential small New England town—something you would expect to see on a postcard—all the improvements that the townspeople would normally make ceased. No painting was done. No repairs were made to buildings, roads, or sidewalks. Day after day, the town grew shabbier and shabbier. People were still living there, but something had changed. What was it?

The town had been proposed as the site for a large hydroelectric plant. A dam was to be built across the river, which would result in the town ultimately being completely submerged. When the project was announced, the people were given many months to arrange their affairs and relocate. But long before most of the people moved away, long before the waters came, the town looked abandoned. One of the citizens was interviewed by the local paper and offered this insight: "Where there is no hope in the future, there is no power in the present."

The Legacy Question

What will matter in the end is one of the most critical questions for a person to answer. It is a question of legacy. Maybe more aptly put, the question is, "How is God inviting me to live right now in light of what will matter the most in the end?"

Once the people of that town realized that none of their efforts would matter in the end, they stopped making improvements altogether. Likewise in our own lives, it's a clear picture of what will matter in the end that helps us to prioritize what we must do now.

Everybody leaves a legacy in life. It might be good or bad or a mixture of the two. We often think of a legacy as something we leave all at once, but that's an inheritance. A legacy is something we are leaving every single day. We build our legacy by the decisions we make; they determine who we become and what we do with our lives.

The legacy question is so durable that it is often revisited throughout life, especially at crossroads moments. The earlier you are compelled by the question, the better. Its answer will not only help you know what to do today, it will also provide you with an anchor against the toss and turn of the tyranny of the urgent.

Being busy and being faithful are not necessarily the same thing. Urgent things are not always the most important things. But they demand immediate attention, so one of the critical tasks for all of us is to carve space and margin to answer and review the legacy question regularly.

How you answer the legacy question actually contains the unexpected power to change the decisions you make today. We are all trading our lives for something. All of this can feel a bit overwhelming until we remember that in Christ, we can know the One who declares, "I make known the end from the beginning" (Isaiah 46:10, NIV). We are not left to answer the legacy question alone; God will help us as we seek him earnestly through things like prayer, Scripture, fasting, solitude, and wise counsel.

The Bible gives us four principles that will help us when it comes to answering what will matter in the end and living now with that in mind. Abiding by these guideposts will help set the stage for not just a wise answer, but a wise life.

Your Legacy Doesn't Begin with You

Every legacy has a beginning, but yours does not begin with you. The word *legacy* means a gift by the decision of another that affects your present reality in a tangible way. During Jesus' day, as previously mentioned, the word *gospel* was usually reserved for the rise of a political ruler or a military victor. Those rulers had people, called "legates," who went on missions as ambassadors for the ruler. So then, a legate was a person sent into the world as a messenger of a gospel.

Without the gospel, there is no legate and no legacy.

Like *Trinity*, the word *legacy* is never actually used in the Bible, but the idea is everywhere. Jesus was clear that he was sending out his followers as his legates. He prayed to God the Father, "As you sent me into the world, I have sent them into the world" (John 17:18, NIV). Writing to the church in Corinth, Paul picks up the same theme, summarizing the gospel of Jesus as the ultimate gift by the decision of Another that affects our present (and future) reality, and then declaring that "we are therefore Christ's ambassadors, as though God were making his appeal through us" (2 Corinthians 5:17-20, NIV).

Our legacy will be the ways in which we first experience that the gospel of Jesus is true, real, and powerful, and then contend for others to know and experience the same. In that sense, our legacy does not begin with what we do; it begins with what Jesus has done.

Your Legacy Is Detected, Not Determined

When I was growing up, I was told a lie. I remember my mom telling me this lie, but then my teachers also lied to me. They were well-intentioned, but it was a lie nonetheless: "You can do anything you put your mind to."

Have you ever been told that lie? How did I discover they were lying to me? On the basketball court, that's how.

I played YMCA basketball. Little kids like me would play on one court; high school kids would play on another court nearby. As a chubby ten-year-old, I watched as an eighteen-year-old took a running start, leaped from the foul line, flew through the air, and dunked the basketball on a ten-foot-high hoop.

It was stunning.

I said in my little chubby heart: *One day, I will be able to do that because my teachers and my mom have told me I can do anything I put my mind to.* Fast-forward twenty-nine years. I am 5′9″ on days I wear my tall shoes. I can't palm a basketball. Let's just say I was probably never intended to dunk on a ten-foot-high rim—let alone from the foul line—no matter how much dear ol' mom believes in me.

Because our legacy does not begin with us, it cannot be based on simply what we set our mind to do. Reading the story of the great leaders of the Bible, from Abraham to Moses to David to the prophets to the disciples, it's clear that for almost all of them, the legacy question was not simply what they set their mind to do. Detecting your unique purpose is more of an art than a science. For some, it will include matching your particular gifts with the opportunities before you to make a difference. For others, it will be the affirmation of a believing community around you who see something in you that you might not yet see in yourself. For some, it will be a sense of passion that stirs you to holy action. For still others, the mission you are sent on might be the last thing you can imagine, but an encounter with God in prayer and his Word will give you the courage and conviction to use your life for that specific goal.[1] When we remember that God is interested in helping us know and live out our purpose, we can be at peace as we ask him to reveal it to us. Either our legacy is a partnership with God, or it will not be something that matters in the end.

Once we come to know Christ, we are created anew so that we might do the good works that God has in mind for us to do (see Ephesians 2:8-10). Answering what will matter in the end is less a matter of what we set our minds to and more a matter of discovering what God has in mind for us to do. As neurologist Viktor Frankl once observed, "We do not determine our purpose, we detect it."[2] Once we discern our assignment, a holy urgency compels us to get it done. As Jesus once said, "We must quickly carry out the tasks assigned us by the one who sent us. The night is coming, and then no one can work" (John 9:4).

Your Legacy Will Require a Fight

Fulfilling your legacy will not necessarily be easy. Sometimes it will require endurance and energy, much like being in a fight.

When was the last time you saw a good old-fashioned fistfight? Not a sanctioned sporting event, but in person, up close? For me, it was a time when I had the weekend off. My wife, Allison, and I decided to load up our three kids and make the drive from Los Angeles to a coastal town called San Luis Obispo. The town slogan is "The Happiest Place in America." I have been to several just plain happy places in America, but never to the *happiest* place, so that seemed worth the weekend.

We arrived in the happiest place in America, turned the corner in our minivan, and on the sidewalk we saw two women—one adult, one teenager—pulling each other's hair and throwing fists. Apparently, the term *happiest* must be a relative term.

What would you do when you see that happening? My wife encouraged me to pull over so we could do something— even though we did not exactly know what we would do.

I pulled over and could see the situation in my rearview mirror. They had stopped fighting, and the older woman appeared to be getting back into the car. Instead, she got a can of pepper spray. The teenager backed up, asking her to leave her alone, but the woman blasted the girl with the pepper spray, emptying the can and throwing it down on the sidewalk.

At this point, I was running up the sidewalk, yelling at the woman to stop. The girl was on the ground, screaming, saying she couldn't see, and the woman prepared to start fighting again. So I stepped over the girl and told the woman to back up. It was one of those moments where you wonder, *How did I get here?*

With a wild look in her eye, the woman glared at me like she was trying to make me spontaneously combust. She yelled, "Get back in your car and keep driving. This is none of your business." The girl, apparently the woman's daughter, was still on the ground, gagging from the pepper spray; Allison was now attending to her. The woman made a fist as if she was about to start throwing punches at me, Allison, or her daughter.

By this point, I had two thoughts running through my head, and neither of them was, *What would Jesus do?*

The first thought was, *If this woman attacks her daughter or Allison, she's about to find out how just how well this old rugby player can tackle.*

The second thought was a question: *Would Christian Assembly fire me as their pastor if I got into a street fight?*

Thankfully, the woman decided to back off. The cops had arrived at this point, and we simply gave our statements and then let them handle it from there. Happiness was restored to the happiest place in America.

This story might call into serious question whether I am fit to write a book about following Jesus. I did not start out looking for a fight, but when the moment came, neither could I stomach the idea of allowing the woman to continue to pound her daughter. Our intervention was for the daughter, but also for the mom, that she would not go any further, doing more damage that she might later regret. Sometimes the fight finds you.

Finding something worth fighting for is critical to answering the legacy question. The moment we feel compelled to live for something that will matter in the end is the moment we enter into a spiritual contest just as real as a sidewalk brawl. All Christ-centered leaders have some way that they feel compelled to make tangible the reality of the gospel for those around them. The moment you decide to move from being a spiritual bystander to a spiritual brawler is the moment you become a leader in my eyes. As my friend once told me, "Indifferent people cannot make a difference."[3]

Being in a fight is one of the central metaphors of a faithful life in the New Testament. At one point, Jesus tells a group, "From the time John the Baptist began preaching until now, the Kingdom of Heaven has been forcefully advancing, and violent people are attacking it" (Matthew 11:12). Paul tells Timothy to "fight the good fight for the true faith" (1 Timothy 6:12) and to "fight well in the Lord's battles" (1 Timothy 1:18). Elsewhere we are told that we "are not fighting against flesh-and-blood enemies, but against evil rulers and authorities of the unseen world" (Ephesians 6:12), that we "use God's mighty weapons, not worldly weapons, to knock down the strongholds of human reasoning and to destroy false arguments" (2 Corinthians 10:4), and that as a leader Paul is "not just shadowboxing" (1 Corinthians 9:26).

Not all fighters are leaders, but all leaders in the Kingdom are fighters. What do some of these fights look like? They are almost innumerable. We are not fighting *with* people so much as fighting *for* people, compelled by the love of Christ.[4] The fight might include leading a business, classroom, or home in such a way that people can flourish under the grace of God. It might be creating art, music, or films that inspire others to what is good, right, and true. There may be a particular person you will fight for in prayer, in conversation, and in acts of love, that they might become a devoted follower of Jesus Christ. For still others it might be fighting for a particular injustice to be made right in Jesus' name. It will include feeding the hungry, welcoming the stranger, clothing the naked, visiting the sick and prisoner, and other acts of compassion and faith (Matthew 25:37-40). It may include contending for the truth of the gospel over and against false teachings that are not in line with the reality of the good news. For some, the fight will be starting new local churches or leading existing ones in a dynamic and life-giving way. Since the gospel of Jesus comes to make all things new, the fights that we are called to step into will touch every realm, from business to family to government to the arts to education and beyond. None of us can fight for everything, but all of us can fight for something in Jesus' name.

Once You Know Your Legacy, Stay in Your Lane

Not long ago, I had a conversation with a great young leader. Bo is the lead pastor of our student ministry. He went to witness the installment of one of his friends as the lead pastor of a small church. Bo shared with me the honest feelings that stirred in him as a pastor to students. He had a heart question of whether he should look to move into a similar role. It's a fair question and a good question; it becomes a great question when you bring it to your prayers.

Bo did that, and he had a sense of God giving him the image of a runner in a 100-meter dash, along with the phrase, "Stay in your lane." Bo reflected that runners who step out of their assigned lane are disqualified from the race—even if they finish first. What Bo was saying in essence is that he did not need to compare God's plan for his life with another's life.

Bo is wise beyond his years. Your legacy is unique—not in the sense that no one else will be given a similar assignment, but because *you* are unique; no one else on the planet is capable of doing your assignment in the exact same way.

For example, you might detect that part of your mission, as a legate of the gospel of Jesus Christ, is to fight against a particular injustice in the name of Christ. There may be others who also feel assigned to step into that same fight, but that does not lessen your unique contribution to overturning that injustice. Be certain you stay focused on what God is asking of you.

What will matter in the end is God's prepared way for you to be an ambassador for the gospel of Jesus Christ. It's easy from time to time to suffer from "legacy comparison-itis." This is when we get sidetracked from our purpose because of what is happening in another person's life. Jesus taught on this specifically. At one point, he tells a story of people complaining about their wages after comparing them to what others were being paid. Jesus has the employer say, "I am not being unfair to you, friend. Didn't you agree to work for a denarius?" (Matthew 20:13, NIV). In another case, Jesus and Peter are having a discussion about Peter's future, when Peter asks about his plan for another disciple, "What about him, Lord?" Jesus answers the question with a question, "What is that to you? As for you, follow me" (John 21:18-24). The point is not that we never change roles, jobs, tasks, or assignments. There are seasons for each thing if God reassigns us. The point is we are to be focused on our own legacy, our own assignment. In other words, stay in your lane.

Bringing It All Together

Maybe the best way to bring this all together is through the story of my friend Blythe. She is a twentysomething here in Los Angeles who works in the fashion industry. She loves dresses. She also has a heartfelt compassion for the millions of women and children trapped in the global sex slave trade. So the question that arose for her was, "God, what can I do to help combat this issue?"

The answer Blythe lived her way into at God's leading is something called "Dressember" (www.dressemberfoundation .org). The basic idea was to mobilize women to wear a dress every single day in December, posting a picture on social media. The women would ask friends to sponsor them, with all the money going to reputable organizations that raise awareness and combat the global sex slave trade in Jesus' name.

Guess what happened? Some critics said the idea was foolish, self-promotional. Sometimes your legacy not only requires you to fight injustice, but to also fight against discouragement. She "stayed in her lane" trusting that God would give her the power to endure. Being criticized is not the worst thing that can happen. The worst thing that can happen is to let the critics keep you from living out your legacy.

Blythe stuck with it. What her critics could not understand is that the campaign was not about dresses, fashion, or photos. It was not even about awareness. It was not even about money. The goal was to free women from slavery in Jesus' name.

The grace of God saves us. But then it also changes us. As Tim Keller notes, "There is a direct relationship between a person's grasp and experience of God's grace, and his or her heart for justice and the poor."[5] Blythe's little campaign went viral, with registered participants from thirty-two countries across six continents. Dressember raised $462,000 in a month. All of that money went toward fighting human trafficking in Jesus' name. How many women and girls will be rescued because of that $462,000? A hundred? Five hundred? A thousand? How many of those women and girls will decide to place their faith in Christ? I do not know the exact number, but I do know that because Blythe stepped up in her unique way to answer what will matter in the end, lives are being transformed *now*.

There can be unexpected power from asking God the right questions. They lead to answers you would have thought unbelievable when you first asked him.

No-Regret Legacy-Making

A while back, someone came up with the idea to survey people who were ninety-five years old or older. They did not let any ninety-four-year-old whippersnappers in this survey. The question they asked was this: "As you look back on your life, what do you wish you had done differently?" What do you think the top three answers were?

1. I wish I had reflected more.
2. I wish I had taken more risks.
3. I wish I had lived for something that would outlive me.[6]

When you are ninety-five years old, it will be hard to change your legacy. But my guess is that if you are reading this, then you probably have a few years before you reach that age. Do not waste your life on what will not matter in the end. God has created you and has a special contribution for you to make as part of extending his good news to others. Asking the legacy question now will give you the power to do what

God is asking of you today, and will save you from a list of regrets tomorrow.

Questions Worth Being Curious About

1. If you created a list of things that will matter at the end of your life, what would be on it? Why would you put those things on it? How do those things compare with what God's Word tells us matter most?

2. Does your everyday life reflect your conviction that those things will matter in the end? If not, what can you do to change it? Where do you get pulled into living for things that will not matter in the end? Why is that?

3. How is God asking you to be his ambassador— or legate—in your everyday life? Do you have a sense of that? If so, what step can you take to live into that?

14

FROM CURIOUS FAITH TO WONDROUS JOY: THE DAY WHEN QUESTIONS ARE REPLACED WITH JOY

In that day you will no longer ask me anything.

JESUS, IN JOHN 16:23 (NIV)

[Nearing the end of his time on earth, Jesus told his disciples,]
"In a little while you won't see me anymore. But a little while after
that, you will see me again." Some of the disciples asked each other,
"What does he mean? . . . We don't understand."

JOHN 16:16-18

NOT UNDERSTANDING IS PART of what it means to be a disciple, part of what it means to be curious. It's how faith is formed. It's how trust is built. However, our curiosity is not just with one another. Our questions are asked in the presence of the One who said he was the way, the truth, and the life. He confirmed as much not only with his many miracles, but by his death and resurrection. Jesus showed us that he is the logic we are looking for, our guide in the darkness. We are not alone in our questions. The Word became flesh and dwelt among us.

When Jesus dwelt among us, questions were often the way he led us—not just to new answers, but to new lives, empowered by his work through the Cross and Resurrection. Jesus was telling his disciples that death will have its day, but his death and resurrection would defeat the power of sin and death over us. Curiosity does not save us. Jesus does by his work on the Cross and through the Resurrection if we place our faith and trust in him.

As Jesus' disciples pressed him to explain what he meant, he told them,

> I tell you the truth, you will weep and mourn over
> what is going to happen to me, but the world will
> rejoice. You will grieve, but your grief will suddenly
> turn to wonderful joy. It will be like a woman
> suffering the pains of labor. When her child is born,
> her anguish gives way to joy because she has brought
> a new baby into the world. So you have sorrow now,
> but I will see you again; then you will rejoice, and no
> one can rob you of that joy. At that time you won't
> need to ask me for anything. I tell you the truth,
> you will ask the Father directly, and he will grant
> your request because you use my name. You haven't
> done this before. Ask, using my name, and you will
> receive, and you will have abundant joy.
> JOHN 16:20-24

A curious faith is what we live now, but it's not just a faith of idle questions. We are asking our way to the world God wants.

In that sense, this has been a book on prayer. Curiosity alone is not enough to live out God's plan for us. It takes courage to trust that God's logic will make sense not just as we wrestle with it in our hearts or minds or discuss it with our friends, but when we begin to integrate it into our lives. Questions that we ask in prayer, answers that we live in everyday life. In other words, to ask is to act.

Jesus once told the leading priests and elders a story:

> A man with two sons told the older boy, "Son,
> go out and work in the vineyard today." The son
> answered, "No, I won't go," but later he changed his
> mind and went anyway. Then the father told the
> other son, "You go," and he said, "Yes, sir, I will."
> But he didn't go.
> MATTHEW 21:28-30

Jesus continued, "Which of the two obeyed his father?" The priests and elders replied, "The first" (verse 31). They recognized that while the second son had an answer, it wasn't an answer that mattered because it was left unlived. Too often, we can be like the second son, subverting the work of God in and through us by focusing on answers that don't matter. The great danger of discipleship is that we only intellectualize or spiritualize our questions, rather than incarnating them in our lives.

Jesus often turned intellectual questions into practical questions. When we are led by questions, we do not just indulge them, we live into them, eventually arriving at the best answers, and as a result, our best life. I do not know why the first son changed his mind and went anyway. Jesus does not give us that answer. It's not an answer that matters, actually. The point is that he did, and so can we.

What I've seen in watching thousands of lives unfold is that the most mature followers of Jesus remain curious, even as the nature of the questions change. Initially, the questions of a curious faith center on things such as "Is God real? If so, what is he like? Can he be trusted? If God's good, why is there pain and suffering in the world? Can God's Word be trusted? How and why should I pray?" Not every such question will be so completely answered that we never wonder about it again, but they are answered enough to allow us to keep moving forward as we follow Jesus. As the poet Rainer Maria Rilke once penned, "Live the questions now. Perhaps then, someday far in the future, you will gradually, without even noticing it, live your way into the answer."[1]

In most cases, we return to some of these prayerful questions as life unfolds. Having wrestled with the initial question of why suffering exists, slowly we become curious as to what God is inviting us to do about the suffering around us in our everyday life. Instead of how to articulate an airtight theology of suffering, the curiosity becomes how to live a compassionate life while we await the day when all suffering will cease. Having wrestled with the initial questions of whether prayer matters, we move toward what it might look like to take all matters to God in prayer. The initial questions often center on what I believe; the next set of questions centers on how I will live. In other words, how much of my theology will I have the courage to allow into my autobiography?

When we have a curious faith, we begin to understand that to ask is to act. How I live becomes the clearest indicator of what I actually believe.

Humble curiosity is the foundation of a life-changing faith. Not just a faith that you believe but also a faith that you live. And yet, Jesus is clear that humble curiosity is not the end of the story. There will be a day when we move from curious faith to wondrous joy. One day, God's will *will* be done on earth as it is in heaven. We get tastes of that here and now as we live out God's answers to our questions. Even still, we know that for all who are in Christ, the best is yet to come.

I wonder what that will be like. Are you curious? I am.

ACKNOWLEDGMENTS

Curious would never have seen the light of day without the help of some amazingly talented people. Don Pape's vibrancy and encouragement as the publisher was a critical spark in moving things from idea to reality. David Zimmerman's diligent work editing the manuscript has made the book a wholly better project. Thank you also to the whole team at Tyndale House Publishers who worked on everything from designing the book cover (Dean Renninger and Nicole Grimes) to getting the word out about the book to others (particularly Robin Bermel and Christy Stroud). It's a gift to have the opportunity to work with such diligent and gifted people.

Thank you to the Christian Assembly Church staff team for all the ways that you have shaped the thoughts in this book through our everyday conversations and experiments of what it means to follow Jesus together. Lastly, *Curious* came together at the encouragement of the Christian Assembly Council members who immediately saw the invitation to write a book as part of the ministry of Christian Assembly to the wider body of Christ. Without that, *Curious* would never have been penned.

NOTES

INTRODUCTION
1. Plato, *Apology* 21d.
2. Great books that address those questions: Tim Keller, *The Reason for God* (New York: Riverhead Books, 2009); Lee Strobel, *Case for* series (Grand Rapids: Zondervan); N. T. Wright, *Simply Christian* (San Francisco: HarperOne, 2010); C. S. Lewis, *Mere Christianity* (San Francisco: HarperOne, 2009); and almost any book by Ravi Zacharias, among others.

CHAPTER 1: THE UNEXPECTED POWER OF THE RIGHT QUESTION
1. Here are the four by my count:
   a. "Why couldn't we cast out that demon?" Jesus answered, "You don't have enough faith" (see Matthew 17:19-20).
   b. "How often should I forgive someone who sins against me? Seven times?" Jesus answered, "Seventy times seven!" (see Matthew 18:21-22).
   c. "Of all the commandments, which is the most important?" Jesus answered, "The most important commandment is this: 'Listen, O Israel! The Lord our God is the one and only Lord. And you must love the Lord your God with all your heart, all your soul, all your mind, and all your strength.' The second is equally important: 'Love your neighbor as yourself.' No other commandment is greater than these" (see Mark 12:28-31).
   d. "Are you the Messiah, the Son of the Blessed One?" Jesus answered, "I Am" (see Mark 14:61-62).
      You could possibly include a fifth question—Jesus' chapter-long response to his disciples' question about the end of the world (see Matthew 24:3-51), but he is not nearly as direct in that response as he is in the four above.

2. John Dear, *The Questions of Jesus* (New York: Doubleday, 2004), 2.
3. John Claypool, *Stories Jesus Still Tells* (Lanham, MD: Rowman & Littlefield, 2007), 84.
4. Thomas Merton, *A Thomas Merton Reader*, ed. Thomas P. McDonnell (New York: Doubleday, 1989), 213.
5. Chris Brady and Orrin Woodward, *Launching a Leadership Revolution* (New York: Hachette, 2005), 28–29.
6. "Can you drink the cup I drink or be baptized with the baptism I am baptized with?" (Mark 10:38, NIV).
7. C. S. Lewis, *God in the Dock* (Grand Rapids, MI: Eerdmans, 2014), 90–91.

CHAPTER 2: UNINTENDED PRETENDERS

1. Roman Catholics tend to understand this verse as establishing the leadership of Peter. Protestants tend to believe that in saying this, Jesus was identifying himself as the Messiah. But in either case, it's clear that Peter is seen as a leader even among the group of twelve.
2. Bill Hybels, Willow Creek Global Leadership Summit, Chicago, Illinois, 2009.
3. Paul Vitello, "Taking a Break from the Lord's Work," *New York Times*, August 1, 2010.
4. Vitello, "Taking a Break."
5. Vitello, "Taking a Break."
6. Hyrum Smith, quoted in Chris Brady and Orrin Woodward, *Launching a Leadership Revolution* (New York: Hachette, 2005), 7.
7. Some people believe that the words are interchangeable, but I don't find the reasoning compelling. In addition, they provide no real explanation why Peter becomes saddened by Jesus' change of word in the final question.
8. Frederick Danker, ed., *A Greek-English Lexicon of the New Testament and Other Early Christian Literature*, 3rd ed. (Chicago: University of Chicago Press, 2000).
9. The root word is the same. Jesus uses the second-person suffix ending, where Peter uses the first-person suffix ending.

CHAPTER 3: A COMMUNITY OF CO-CONSPIRATORS

1. Brenda Gazzar, "Los Angeles County First in the Nation to 10 Million People," *Los Angeles Daily News*, December 12, 2013, http://www.dailynews.com/social-affairs/20131212/los-angeles-county-first-in-the-nation-to-10-million-people.

2. Los Angeles Homeless Services Authority, *2013 Los Angeles Homeless Count,* documents.lahsa.org/planning/homelesscount/2013/HC13-Results -LACounty-COC-Nov2013.pdf. These numbers include those sleeping on private property with permission to stay no more than ninety days.

3. Los Angeles Homeless Services Authority, *2013 Los Angeles Homeless Count.*

4. Matthew 14:15-21. It's helpful to note that one of the miraculous feedings was on the Jewish side of the Sea of Galilee with a largely Jewish crowd. The other miraculous feeding was on the Gentile side of the lake with a largely Gentile crowd. Jesus is communicating that he is the Bread of Life for both sides of the lake—Jews and Gentiles.

5. Jesus goes on to ask them, "'Why can't you understand that I'm not talking about bread? So again I say, "Beware of the yeast of the Pharisees and Sadducees."' Then at last they understood that he wasn't speaking about the yeast in bread, but about the deceptive teaching of the Pharisees and Sadducees" (Matthew 16:11-12).

6. "Adult Learning Theory and Principles," from QOTFC: The Clinical Educator's Resource Kit, http://www.qotfc.edu.au/resource/?page=65375.

7. Jud Wilhite, Exponential Conference, Orlando, Florida, 2012.

CHAPTER 4: THE FOUNDATIONAL QUESTION

1. Dallas Willard, *Renovation of the Heart* (Colorado Springs: NavPress, 2002), 111, italics in the original.

2. Tim Keller, "Gospel-Centered Ministry," Gospel Coalition Conference, 2007. Keller is quoting David Martyn Lloyd-Jones (www.keylife.org /articles/good-news-vs-good-advice).

3. *Priene* 105.40.

4. John Ortberg, quoting Dallas Willard, in *Soul Keeping* (Grand Rapids, MI: Zondervan, 2014), 191.

5. Willard, *Renovation of the Heart*, 130, italics in the original.

6. James Choung has a great way to explain the gospel using four circles. You can read about it in his book *True Story: A Christianity Worth Believing In* (Downers Grove, IL: InterVarsity Press, 2008).

7. N. T. Wright, quoted in Shawn Kennedy, "What Is the Gospel?" www.gcdiscipleship.com/what-do-we-mean-when-we-say-the-gospel/.

8. Justin Buzzard, twitter.com/justinbuzzard.

CHAPTER 5: THE IDENTITY QUESTION

1. Wayne Cordeiro, Exponential Conference, Orlando, Florida, 2012.

2. Henry Cloud and John Townsend, *Boundaries* (Grand Rapids, MI: Zondervan, 1992), 66.

3. Cloud and Townsend, *Boundaries*, 66.
4. John Ortberg, *Soul Keeping* (Grand Rapids: Zondervan, 2014), 167.
5. Tim Keller, *Jesus the King* (New York: Penguin, 2011).
6. I first heard this quote from my father-in-law.
7. Henri Nouwen, *Life of the Beloved* (New York: Crossroads, 1992), 21.
8. Quoted in Chris Brady and Orrin Woodward, *Launching a Leadership Revolution* (New York: Hachette, 2005), 9.
9. Janet Lowe, ed., *Warren Buffet Speaks* (New York: John Wiley & Sons, 1997), 69.
10. The word *authority* in Greek is the combination of "out of" and a form of the root word for "I Am." In other words, genuine authority comes out of the I Am. I Am Who I Am is the name that God reveals for himself to Moses in Exodus 3:14 (NIV).
11. Frank Laubach, *Man of Prayer* (Syracuse, NY: Laubach Literacy International, 1990), 154.

CHAPTER 6: THE DISCERNMENT QUESTION
1. John Ortberg, "Rich Dad, Poor Dad," sermon from Menlo Park Presbyterian Church podcast, June 23, 2014.
2. Paul Nutt, "Surprising but True: Half the Decisions in Organizations Fail," *Academy of Management Executive* 13 (1999): 75–90.
3. Nutt, "Surprising but True."
4. Ignatius's insights are beyond the scope of this chapter. However, I encourage you to check out Larry Warner, *Journey with Jesus* (Downers Grove, IL: InterVarsity Press, 2010), which helps make the spiritual exercises of Ignatius accessible to people today. Those exercises often deal with discernment.

CHAPTER 7: THE RECOVERY QUESTION
1. Mauricio's story is used by permission. Curious to know more? Visit www.treeoflife84.com.

CHAPTER 8: THE COMMUNITY QUESTION
1. My thanks to Greg Surratt for this illustration idea.
2. Janet Lowe, ed., *Warren Buffet Speaks* (New York: John Wiley & Sons, 1997), 22.
3. E-mail correspondence with the author. Reprinted here by permission.
4. Quoted in Beau Hughes, "Awaiting Redemption, Part One: Work," (sermon, The Village Church, February 24, 2008), http://www.thevillage

church.net/media/sermons/transcripts/200802241100DWC21ASAAA
_BeauHughes_AwaitingRedemptionPt1-Work.pdf.

CHAPTER 9: THE MULTI-ETHNIC QUESTION

1. This goes back to the identity question from the earlier chapter.
2. *Los Angeles Times* Mapping Project, maps.latimes.com/neighborhoods
/neighborhood/eagle-rock/.

CHAPTER 10: THE MULTI-GENERATIONAL QUESTION

1. "Choose One Chair," *Guideposts*, February 2, 2009, posted to Bible.org,
https://bible.org/illustration/choose-one-chair.
2. "Southern Baptists Face Further Decline Without Renewed Evangelism
Emphasis," *Florida Baptist Witness*, July 28, 2009, quoted in James Emery
White, *What They Didn't Teach You in Seminary* (Grand Rapids, MI: Baker,
2011), 74.
3. This quote has been attributed to both Henrietta Mears and Howard
Hendricks. It could be that Mears said it first and that Hendricks
repeated it.
4. Larry Osborne, Southern California Young Lead Pastors Gathering, 2013.
5. For example, see Exodus 12:42; 29:42; Esther 9:28; Psalm 78:4.

CHAPTER 11: THE LOCAL QUESTION

1. Walter Hamilton, "Eagle Rock Named Second 'Hottest' Neighborhood
in U.S.," *Los Angeles Times*, January 15, 2014.
2. *Los Angeles Times* Mapping Project, http://maps.latimes.com
/neighborhoods/neighborhood/eagle-rock/.

CHAPTER 12: THE GLOBAL QUESTION

1. *Ethne* is the Greek word translated as "nations" in Matthew 24:14. It
means "peoples" or "tribes" rather than "countries."
2. "The Amazing Countdown Facts," US Center for World Mission, *Mission
Frontiers* (September–October 2009), 30, http://joshuaproject.net/assets
/media/assets/articles/amazing-countdown-facts.pdf.
3. "The Amazing Countdown," 32.
4. Patrick Johnstone and Jason Mandryk, *Operation World* (Tyrone, GA:
Authentic Media, 2005), 7.
5. David B. Barrett and Todd M. Johnson, *World Christian Trends AD 30—
AD 2200: Interpreting the Annual Christian Megacensus* (Pasadena, CA:
William Carey Library, 2001), 656.

6. "General Statistics," The Traveling Team, www.thetravelingteam.org/stats.
7. Kit Yarrow, "Millions on Pet Halloween Costumes? Why We Spend More and More on Pets," *Time*, October 4, 2012, http://business.time.com/2012/10/04/millions-on-pet-halloween-costumes-why-we-spend-more-and-more-on-pets/.
8. "General Statistics," The Traveling Team, www.thetravelingteam.org/stats.
9. "General Statistics," The Traveling Team, www.thetravelingteam.org/stats.
10. "General Statistics," The Traveling Team, www.thetravelingteam.org/stats.

CHAPTER 13: THE LEGACY QUESTION

1. Moses had this experience. So did Gideon, among others.
2. Chris Brady and Orrin Woodward, *Launching a Leadership Revolution* (New York: Hachette, 2005), 39.
3. Enock De Assis, sermon, Christian Assembly Church, spring 2014.
4. Neither should we be naive. Sometimes we will have to fight with people to overturn injustice. For example, undoing the sex slave trade will require standing against those who profit from the sale of women and children for pleasure. We can do this through prayer, public pressure, and legal actions to close down brothels.
5. Tim Keller. *Generous Justice: How God's Grace Makes Us Just* (New York: Penguin, 2010), xix.
6. Tony Campolo, *Who Switched the Price Tags?* (Nashville: Thomas Nelson, 2008), 26–27.

CHAPTER 14: FROM CURIOUS FAITH TO WONDROUS JOY

1. Rainer Maria Rilke, *Letters to a Young Poet #4* (New York: Random House, 1984).

ABOUT THE AUTHOR

TOM HUGHES grew up in Pittsburgh, Pennsylvania. After study-ing world religions, sociology, and environmental studies at Ohio Wesleyan University, he was headed to law school when God inter-vened, sending him into ministry full-time.

Tom launched and led a student ministry on the East Coast for a number of years before moving to England to study with the missional church movement. From there Tom moved to Pasadena, California, to earn his Master of Divinity degree at Fuller Theological Seminary.

Tom and his wife, Allison, discovered Christian Assembly (CA) in 2002 when a neighbor invited them to come and check it out. In 2003, Tom joined the CA staff as part of the teach-ing team, with the specific assignment to reach young adults. In 2007, Tom became co-lead pastor there. He is also co-catalyst of the Los Angeles Church Planting Movement (www.lacpm.org), a coordinated initiative to plant a gospel-driven church in every neighborhood in metro Los Angeles.

Tom is a rabid Pittsburgh Steelers fan who loves the mountains and still enjoys kicking the soccer ball around from time to time. He and Allison have three children: Caleb, Sophia, and Micah.

BUILDING CHURCHES
THAT MAKE DISCIPLES

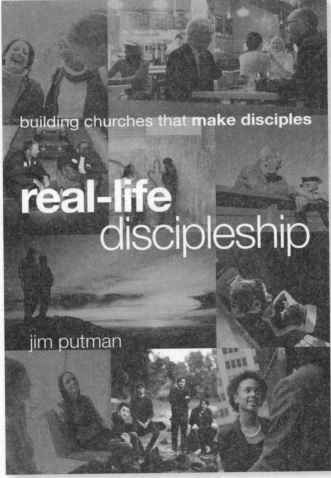

building churches that **make disciples**

real-life
discipleship

jim putman

ISBN 978-1-61521-560-7

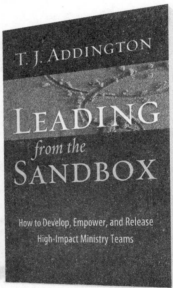